TIPS FOR TEACHING
INTRODUCTORY
SOCIOLOGY

Jerry M. Lewis
Kent State University

West Publishing Company
Minneapolis/St. Paul • New York
Los Angeles • San Francisco

WEST'S COMMITMENT TO THE ENVIRONMENT

In 1906, West Publishing Company began recycling materials left over from the production of books. This began a tradition of efficient and responsible use of resources. Today, up to 95% of our legal books and 70% of our college texts and school texts are printed on recycled, acid-free stock. West also recycles nearly 22 million pounds of scrap paper annually—the equivalent of 181,717 trees. Since the 1960s, West has devised ways to capture and recycle waste inks, solvents, oils, and vapors created in the printing process. We also recycle plastics of all kinds, wood, glass, corrugated cardboard, and batteries, and have eliminated the use of Styrofoam book packaging. We at West are proud of the longevity and the scope of our commitment to the environment.

Production, Prepress, Printing and Binding by West Publishing Company.

 TEXT IS PRINTED ON 10% POST CONSUMER RECYCLED PAPER    PRINTED WITH SOY INK™

COPYRIGHT © 1995 by WEST PUBLISHING CO.
610 Opperman Drive
P.O. Box 64526
St. Paul, MN 55164–0526

ISBN 0–314–04906–1

CONTENTS

PREFACE

This monograph is the product of a long career in sociology teaching. I am indebted to a number of people and institutions for their help and support.

Normally one thanks one's spouse last. However, my wife, Diane, a dedicated and creative introductory sociology teacher, deserves recognition and appreciation for her impact on this monograph. She has provided me with considerable help and insight in teaching of family and socialization particularly in a cross-cultural context. She has given me many suggestions on how to make the introductory course more humane.

In addition, I want to identify and thank, with deep appreciation, the following people and organizations:

Professor Denzel Benson, Kent State University, with whom I have written on student evaluations and who is the coauthor of Section Eight of this monograph.

Professors Joan Morris, University of Central Florida and Anne Hendershott, University of San Diego, with whom I have often talked about the importance of the introductory course. Both have helped me in my writing on the use of class projects in the introductory course.

Professor Bebe Lavin, my chair for over a decade, with whom I have had many interesting discussions of the teaching of the mass sections of the introductory course.

Professor Tom Korllos, Kent State University, for his ideas on creating community in the introductory course.

Professors Norm Duffy, Chemistry, and Tom Hensley, Political Science, of Kent State University are award winning teachers. I have had many interesting and creative talks with them on the importance of undergraduate teaching.

Alan Maclear, York High School, Elmhurst, Illinois who, in 1955, first stimulated my interest in sociology in his "Senior Sociology" class and J. Harold Ennis, my advisor at Cornell College in Mt. Vernon Iowa who helped me sustain it.

Janell Lewis, my daughter, took "intro" with me at Kent State and graduated with a major in sociology. She read and helpfully commented on an earlier version of the manuscript.

Jeanne Mekolichick, my graduate assistant, provided substantive and editorial comments on an earlier version of the manuscript.

Mrs. Janice Puckett and Mrs. Linda Mauck for their careful work in preparing the manuscript.

West Publishers for its encouragement and willingness to publish this monograph.

v

Many hundreds of introductory students have listened to me and provided feedback. I have tried to listen and I hope future generations of introductory students have profited from these responses.

This monograph is dedicated to my University of Illinois advisor--Professor Bernard Farber.

SECTION ONE
INTRODUCTION

On the Importance of the Introductory Course

There is no more important course than "Introduction to Sociology." It is important to the student while being the lifeblood of the department and the discipline. It should receive the best that any instructor has to give. "Intro," sometimes called "Principles of Sociology," is important for three reasons. First, it makes the college student aware of how sociologists approach intellectual questions. Often this idea is expressed by saying the "Intro" course gives the beginning student a chance to develop a "sociological imagination." C. Wright Mills' terms, the sociological imagination is a way of thinking which focuses on the effort to understand the intersections of a person's biography and history within society. (Mills, 1959, p. 7). In other words, to develop a sociological imagination is to develop a methodology for thinking about one's social structural experiences and situations.

The sociological imagination includes two basic cognitive processes, both of which need to be carefully developed by the beginning student. The first is theoretical thinking about social structure while the second is the place of empirical inquiry in sociological analysis. Thus, the beginning sociology student should come away from the "Intro" class respecting theoretical approaches as well as prepared to evaluate and use empirical evidence.

Second, while it is true that many students do not go beyond the introductory class in their educational activities, some students do. Many universities have general education

1

requirements that call for a second or even a third sociology course to meet the distributive requirements. The second course is often social problems or social psychology. Whatever it is, the introductory teacher has a responsibility to prepare his students for further study using sociological theory and methods. Another way that students continue their study of sociology is to take a course related to their field or major requirements. For example, often nursing students may be required to take a sociology of health course or journalism students a course in collective behavior. Sometimes students take their statistics in sociology. These courses are typically taught as upper-division courses. Thus, instructors teaching the beginning course need to be concerned about preparing their students for upper level work. Lastly, Introduction to Sociology students carry on their sociological education by either minoring or majoring in this subject. The fact that we are teaching potential majors should serve to challenge us to prepare our students well in terms of theory and methods. Ask yourself: What if you had a student in an upper division course who had never heard of Durkheim, Weber or Marx? What if this student did not know what a random sample was or an interval measure? You would mentally ask: With whom did you have "Intro"?

Third, sociology fits in the general liberal arts perspective that students should be broadly educated to better function as citizens in American society or the world. The beginning student should come away with a sense of social structure and a respect for the place of evidence in decision making. All this shows that the Introduction to Sociology course is very important. It is a serious responsibility that the instructor should not take lightly. It is my wish that this volume will help you in the exciting venture of teaching beginning sociology to your students.

Plan of the Monograph

Tips for Teaching Introductory Sociology (**TIPSTEACH**), is divided into nine more sections. Section Two discusses course goals by drawing on ASA material on this issue. The place of the syllabus in creating a contract for reaching course goals concludes this section. Section Three discusses the lecture in sociological teaching while Section Four presents outlines for nine core lectures in beginning sociology. Section Five discusses examinations associated with teaching beginning sociology.

Section Six reviews active learning exercises for stimulating participation and discussion in the introductory course. Section Seven describes how the field research project can be integrated into the beginning course. Section Eight explores the terrors of course evaluations for the new instructor of the introductory course and tries to reduce them. Section Nine deals with a particular interest of mine - the use of humor in teaching the introductory course and prepares the way for the next section on teaching evaluations. Section Ten shows you the external resources that can help you improve your introductory teaching. Section Eleven looks at the role of the sociologist outside the classroom. Twelve concludes the monograph.

Readers of **TIPSTEACH** should feel free to use any of the ideas presented here without cost. I hope that West Publishing Company and ideas in the monograph will help you with your teaching of the Introduction to Sociology course. Should you write anything drawing on these ideas use the normal citation protocols of any academic journal.

My Background

I see this monograph as a conversation between an experienced "Introduction to Sociology" teacher and one who is beginning the adventure of bringing students to sociology. I think it is important to tell you a little about myself.

I joined the Kent State University faculty in 1966 as an ABD from the University of Illinois in Urbana. I received the Ph.D. in 1970 with earlier degrees from Boston University (1963-M.S.) and Cornell College (1959-B.A.).

Kent State University was founded in 1910 as a College and became a University in 1935 when it expanded beyond its original teacher-training goals. It is located in northeastern Ohio. It is roughly 470 miles (about 760 kilometers) west of New York City and about 40 miles southeast of Cleveland, Ohio. Kent State University (KSU) consists of the main campus plus seven regional campuses. The main campus in Kent, Ohio is a large, wooded campus on about 1,200 acres of slightly rolling land. The university is so large that it operates a bus system.

The Kent campus offers baccalaureate, masters and doctoral study programs while the regional campuses offer associate (two year) degrees as well as basic courses for the foundation of finishing a degree at the main campus.

Although Kent has many fine programs, graduates over 3,800 each year, and has an international reputation in such fields as liquid crystals, architecture, and psychology, to name the main ones, it was not until the tragedy of May 4, 1970 that the name of the school was heard throughout the world. That was when four students were killed and nine wounded by the National Guard firing 67 rounds in 13 seconds over the heads of and directly at the array of students that were either protesting, observing, or just passing by the area.

My research is in two areas. First, there is collective behavior where I have conducted studies related to sports crowd violence. Earlier, I wrote on the Kent State tragedy. Second, popular culture studies with a focus on the sociology of film. I have taught a variety of Introduction to Sociology courses including the mass sections with enrollments of over 600 students as well as smaller sections on regional campuses that often have nontraditional students. I lectured to European students in Belgium and England. I polished my "Intro" skills by teaching it at an elite liberal arts college--Cornell College in Mt Vernon, Iowa. I began my introductory teaching career as a teaching assistant at the University of Illinois working on a course that was broadcast on television and radio. In 1976 I received Kent State's College of Art and Sciences outstanding teacher award and in 1983 I was honored to receive the University's Distinguished Teaching Award.

Let's sit down, have a cup of coffee, and begin the adventure of talking about teaching the "Intro" course.

SECTION TWO
COURSE GOALS AND SYLLABI

Introduction

In this section of **TIPSTEACH**, I discuss two important issues related to teaching the introductory course. First, is the process of setting of course goals. Second, and tied to course goals, is the syllabus. This section considers the place of the syllabus in the organization of the course as it moves toward course goals. It looks at the process of setting goals in relation to the sociological imagination as well as general principles of liberal education. The chapter continues with an analysis of the syllabus as a contract. It concludes with a review of two basic types of syllabi - the overview and the detailed.

Setting Course Goals

The American Sociological Association published, under the auspices of the Association of American Colleges, *Liberal Learning and the Sociology Major*. This report took a frank look at the sociology major in the United States and found it wanting. It proposed, in the context of the assessment movement, ways to improve the sociology major. In particular the ASA Report (1991: 9-11) suggested that departments should be guided by three goals in developing and improving the sociology major. First, the creation of the sociological perspective. Second, a concern for linking the sociology major to the general goals of liberal arts education. Third, focusing on the intellectual ability of students by encouraging them to express ideas in written and oral forms. While these perspectives were developed for the major, they are appropriate for any sociology course including the introductory course.

The Sociological Imagination

Departments have defined the sociological perspective as the sociological imagination which is the development of a methodology for thinking about social structure using theory and empirical data.

Most sociologists have a favorite theoretical perspective be it functionalism, conflict or interactionism or some combination of all three. Yet, we have an obligation to teach all theoretical perspectives in a fair and objective manner as unpleasant as that might be for some perspectives.

The typical introduction textbook hits the student with a bewildering body of material very quickly. Texts contain the "Big Three" of theoretical perspectives, structural-functionalism, conflict and interactionism, often adding social exchange theory. The professor has to think through how he or she is going to deal with this problem. It seems to me that teaching any theoretical perspective requires that the professor helps the students understand three basic things. First, certain scholars are identified as exemplars for a theoretical perspective. For example, Emile Durkheim is linked to structural-functionalism, Karl Marx with conflict theory and George Herbert Mead with interactionism. Second, every theoretical perspective has core ideas that are essential to the understanding of the theory. For example, in functionalism the instructor will want to discuss manifest and latent functions while in conflict theory the issue of differential power is key to the understanding of this perspective. Interactionism calls for an evaluation of notions of the self. You must convince your students that an understanding of these core concepts is central to the utilization of the theory. As you teach these ideas remember that beginning sociological students are prone to psychological reductionism and you must continually encourage them to think at the structural or group level of analysis. Third, these theories have been used in analytical work. Try to give your students examples of how sociologists have used particular theoretical approaches to study a specific sociological question. For example, I use Durkheim's structural-functional model of suicide to explain Kamikaze pilots in World War II. (See Lecture 1, p. 37) More materials on achieving these goals are presented in Section Three on lecturing and Section Four with core lecture outlines.

General Goals of Liberal Education

The general goals of a liberal education vary from one educational organization to another, and the teacher of "Intro" should consult his or her college or university's policies.

But, as a rule of thumb, the goals of liberal education typically focus on developing student skills in these areas: independent thinking, developing aesthetic awareness, cultivating a moral and/or ethical system of values, welcoming diversity and committing to value of life long learning.

No "Intro" course could adequately discuss all issues related to these skills. But, there are areas where a start could be made. To get students to become independent thinkers, they should realize soon that sociology is an integrated body of thought about social structure. The sociologist should show students how sociology ties into other courses within the department. For example, when I lecture on socialization I tell my students that my department has a course that investigates this subject in more detail called "Social Psychology." This points to the fact that the instructor of "Intro" should be familiar with other course offerings in the department. Many students tell me that they took further sociology courses because of a good experience with their beginning course. But, sad to say, other students say the opposite.

Regarding aesthetic awareness, an introduction to sociology should encourage students to be introspective which gets them thinking about their own socialization. This, in turn, can get students to value differences in others therefore encouraging an appreciation for differing aesthetic values. Such an appreciation can encourage an appreciation for cultural diversity. We should ask the student to examine the impact of social institutions on their lives. I have used the following handout in both "Intro" and Social Psychology to encourage students to be introspective about their socialization experiences. I use this work sheet several ways. First, in the first class of the semester as an icebreaker. Here the students work with other people in the class helping each other fill out the sheet. Or, at the beginning of the socialization lectures to get my students thinking about this process. Sometimes, I have my students use the work sheet to interview a family member for information about their answers for the "six years old" category. My students tell me that it often gets some interesting conversations going with their family. Third, the introductory sociology course should show students how different value systems can be studied scientifically. When we focus on the religious institution, for example, we can point out how religious practices influence work practices using Weber's thesis and different religious traditions. This also encourages an appreciation for diversity.

Lastly, regarding lifelong learning, the "Intro" course should not be taught in a social science vacuum. The course should be linked to other social science programs. For example, when I lecture on culture, I point out the work of my anthropology colleagues. Or, when discussing the political institution, I name professors in the Political Science Department who have courses dealing with the matters under examination. We sociologists are never hurt when our students take further social science courses wherever they are located.

    I think good social science not only begets more social science but, further, it builds an appreciation for lifelong learning that can be expressed by taking more sociology as an adult learner. And I think we all appreciate nontraditional students in our classes. The instructor of the beginning course should think carefully about the goals of the introductory course. What you want to accomplish is an important question raised in connection with the goals of the department, university or the discipline of sociology.

Selecting a Textbook

    After you have thought through course goals, you begin the search for the textbook, which will become an integral part of your course. Working with the book publishers representatives will be of considerable help in the decision making process (See Section Ten).

    There are basically three types of introductory textbooks. There are the megatextbooks that cover the field of sociology from stem to stern. Usually they have from nineteen to twenty-five chapters. These are the big money makers for publishers. They are always supported by elaborate ancillary packages (see Section Three). The second type are core texts which are boiled down versions of the megatextbooks. They are shorter and are often used in connection with readers of sociological monographs. The third form of the textbook are readers which are used either alone or to support a textbook. Readers contain sociological articles that have stood the test of time in terms of quality or deal with subjects that have not been studied by anyone else. After selecting a textbook, the next step is writing of the syllabi.

FIGURE I

SOCIALIZATION WORK SHEET

EVENT	AGE		
	Six	Twelve	Eighteen
BEST FAMILY TRIP:			
FAVORITE TV SHOW:			
BEST FRIEND:			
FAVORITE TEACHER:			
FAVORITE MOVIE:			
FAVORITE JOKE:			

The Syllabus as Contract

Syllabi are the codification of course goals. But, as we shall see shortly, they are much more. The word "syllabus" derives from the Latin "sillybus" meaning a list and the Greek "sillybos" meaning a parchment label. Today, the word means, in English, an outline of a course of study. In recent years it has also taken on a legalistic meaning. Most students today view the syllabus as a contract. And, they are correct. It is an agreement between the instructor and his or her students about course expectations. But, it is also a road map showing when the intellectual journey is going to begin and end and where some "potholes" (exams) are located. It is very important that the introductory instructor design a syllabus that he or she can follow without getting too far off the track. Students, particularly beginning students, really appreciate organizational predictability in a course. I encourage you to put considerable thought into the syllabi you are developing. Everett Wilson, a sociologist at the University of North Carolina in Chapel Hill, is a veteran observer of teaching trends in sociology. He (Wilson, 1990) created a checklist for reviewing syllabi for his students in his graduate seminar on teaching sociology. He separates the checklist into nine parts which I have considerably modified into five core parts:

1.   The Introductory Course and the Discipline of Sociology
2.   Student's Life Space
3.   Examinations
4.   Active versus Passive Learning
5.   Classroom operations

The Introductory Course and the Discipline of Sociology

Ideally, syllabi should flow from the course goals that have been previously developed. But, like many ideals this is often not so. It is more likely an interactive process. Ask yourself these questions:

1.   Does the syllabus reflect the sociological imagination?
2.   How does a syllabus reflect the goals of general liberal education?
3.   Does the syllabus show that there will be opportunities for written and oral presentations?

The first question suggests that your course and the syllabus that organizes it should have some sense of how to help students develop their sociological imaginations. In practical terms, this means that students should have some sense of their place in the social structure. Your syllabus should reflect the notion that you are going to give your students a chance to be introspective about how culture, social structure and groups shape their lives. Your syllabus should show that you are also going to give your students a sense of the discipline of sociology as well.

The second question puts the introductory course into the liberal education process. At many colleges and universities the introductory sociology course helps meet liberal education or distributive education requirements. Syllabi can reflect this in two ways. First, it should show how this course relates to distributive requirements and, second, how it ties into other social sciences. On this latter point, most textbooks link sociology to other disciplines. You can build lectures on this from your introductory texts treatment of other disciplines. For example, you might take an important issue such as health care and show how different disciplines might examine the issue.

The third question refers to issues that go beyond examinations. Does your course provide opportunities for written and oral presentations? This is essential for all courses.

Lastly, you should put the course goals on the syllabus. Perhaps not in the elaborated form presented here, but perhaps in a summary way at the end to the syllabus.

Work Load and the Student's Life Space

Everett Wilson makes the excellent point that professors should be sensitive to the student culture. After all, we are sociologists. Reading the student newspaper soon after it comes out is a good way to start.

One very insensitive thing teachers do is schedule quizzes, tests and examinations against student culture. While there is probably no perfect day for a test, there are probably some days that are better than others. Don't give a test on a day that is, for some reason, unrealistic for you or your students. I recommend that you be sensitive to the student culture when you schedule a test although not all professors would agree with this. For example, it doesn't make sense to me to have a test on the Monday after Thanksgiving or Spring break or the Friday before Homecoming.

Wilson stresses that the calendar of the course should be clear and precise on the syllabus. Don't schedule a test for the "week of," but give the exact day. This is true for all the events of the course including the due days for: abstracts, laboratory reports, book reviews and projects assignments.

Examinations

I say much more about examinations in Section Five, but for purposes of the syllabus, the form of the test, i.e. multiple-choice, essay, take-home, or open book, should be stated. Second, the syllabus should note the material that is going to be covered by test. This includes not only textbook subjects but lectures as well, including handouts. If you plan to do help sessions, you should clearly state the time and place if it is not during the regular time of the class.

Third, there should be an indication of the value of each test including procedures for rewriting or dropping a test.

Lastly, your make up and retake criteria and procedures need to be clearly described. We don't like to do make ups. We often fail to put the procedures on the syllabi. But, since these syllabi are contracts, it is essential that the rules of make ups and retakes be spelled out.

Active versus Passive Learning

Do you remember the best seminar you had in graduate school? It is likely there was considerable give and take between your professor and the students. Your professor gave you positive recognition for your input. This was active learning at its best. It is probably the best way to learn. But, as sociology introductory classes get bigger for reasons of popularity or finances, active learning is threatened.

The proposition often governs our thought: the greater the number of students in a sociology class, the fewer the opportunities for active learning experiences. Common sense says this is true, but as I show in Section Six on projects it is possible to resist this proposition. If you do plan some active learning activities in your course, you probably do not have to put them on the syllabus unless they involve activities outside the class. But, you do have to think through how you are going to use the activities and whether they require any preparation before, i.e. handouts or overheads.

Wilson suggests one dimension of active learning is the conference with the professor. If you think that this is possible with your student population in the class, then this can be a valuable active learning experience. If you plan to use a conference then I suggest you schedule it on the syllabus listing what is expected from students at the conference.

Classroom Operations

Everett Wilson wants us to ask ourselves this question: What alternative to the traditional lectures have you considered for your course?

This divides into two basic categories - audiovisual aids and nonlecture activities including labs, small group seminars, role playing and sociodrama, and demonstrations. I write more about these techniques in later sections of **TIPSTEACH**. But, when you use alternatives to the lecture, as I think you should, the activities should be scheduled in the syllabus.

Sample Syllabi

The ASA handbook on teaching "Intro" has syllabi in it. I encourage you to get this when you start building your course. Syllabi contain seven content categories including: course goals, reading assignments, examination dates, projects, office hours, grading schemes and bibliographies. I give two types of syllabi to my students - an overview and a detailed one. The ones discussed below are used in my large "Intro" (N=600-700+). Each is discussed using the number in the parentheses which, of course, are not on the copies given to my sociology students.

The Overview Syllabus

The overview syllabus is handed out on the first day. It is designed to give the student a quick snapshot of the course. Always identify your department, the date of the course and its title (1,2,3). This material can be helpful for identifying the course in later years. For example, I have been asked to write letters of reference as late as ten years after the student took a course with me.

FIGURE II

OVERVIEW SYLLABUS

(1)   DEPARTMENT OF SOCIOLOGY -- KENT STATE UNIVERSITY

(2)   Fall Semester, 1993

(3)   COURSE: Introduction to Sociology

(4)   INSTRUCTOR: J. M. Lewis, Ph.D., Professor of Sociology

(5)   TEXT: Jon Shepard SOCIOLOGY; Study Guide; and J.M. Lewis, selected reprints.

(6)   TOPIC OUTLINE:

I.	Introduction
II.	The Sociological Imagination
III.	Social Theory
IV.	Research Methods
V.	Culture and Social Structure
VI.	Social Institutions
	A.	Family
	B.	Religion
	C.	Polity
VII.	Collective Behavior
VIII.	Popular Culture

(7)   EVALUATION: Three (3) Multiple Choice Tests -- 100% of your grade.

(8)   OFFICE: 140 Lowry Hall (first building east of Merrill).

(9)   OFFICE HOURS: Monday, 5:00 - 7:00 p.m.
                           Tuesday & Thursday, 8:30 - 10:00 a.m.

(10)   This course is designed to introduce you to the discipline of sociology. You will be expected to read, think and write intelligently about the social experience. It is the wish of the instructor and the course staff that you develop an enthusiasm for sociology's approach to scientific questions.

Students like to know if you have the doctorate (4) because they feel embarrassed if they call you doctor and you don't have one or vice-versa. I include the academic rank because I prefer students call me "Professor" rather than "Doctor". You should do what you feel comfortable with on this matter. Regarding the Textbooks (5), some professors provide a full citation, but I don't think that is necessary since the text is likely to be easily available in the college or university bookstore.

The overview syllabus provides a general picture of the course with an outline of topics (6) that will be studied. In the opening lecture I review the outline describing what will be dealt with under each topic. Yes, my first day is fairly full. I think students should get their money's worth even on the first day. I'll say more about the first day in Sections Four and Six.

The evaluation procedure is spelled out in general terms here (7) and in more detail in the second syllabus. It is very important to describe your examinations and make up procedures in considerable detail. Students can become quite legalistic about this. I provide a handout (not shown) explaining the procedures for examinations and makeups. This may be because of the fact that it is a large course, but the legalistic dimension is becoming a factor in most courses.

Be sure to state clearly where your office is and the time of your office hours (8,9). Students count on this information particularly in emergencies. I like to conclude all my syllabi with some sense of mission flowing from course goals (10).

The Detailed Syllabus

The detailed syllabus is typically handed out on the second or third meeting of the class. As the title shows, it is a statement of course activities. In "Intro", I believe lectures should be self contained and completed in the allotted period. It is easier to set task expectations when you do this. Students are expected to read the relevant chapter before the lecture. That is why the readings are correlated with specific dates (1,2) rather than listing the reading assignments for the week or blocks of weeks as some professors do. This can be done for upper division courses, but does not seem to work for lower division courses such as "Intro". Using films in a course has mixed blessings. Students like films (3), but they often do not see them as "part" of the course, therefore, subject to testing. Listing the showing of a film for a particular day often guarantees higher cutting particularly in large courses. This goes with the pattern that a film is entertainment not serious academic work. On the other hand, there are so many good films available that the professor would shortchange his or her students if some films were not used. I say more about how I use films in the section on lectures.

Dr. J's flea market (4) is a way I get students to ask questions in class and is presented in Section Seven. Practice tests (5) are important because they are a way of getting students to learn your testing procedure. They also have the latent function of encouraging students to begin the review process earlier for the actual test. This is true for a Help session as well (6).

FIGURE III

DETAILED SYLLABUS

(1) DATES (1993) TOPICS AND ASSIGNMENTS

(2) 8-31   Introduction
Reading: Shepard, Chapter 1

9-2   Theory, Part 1
Reading: Shepard, Chapter 2

9-7   Theory, Part 2

9-9   Research Methods, Part 1
Reading: Shepard, Chapter 3

9-14   Research Methods, Part 2
(3)   Film: "Methodology" (cc3114) This film shows the experimental method stressing independent and dependent variables. It is also useful for understanding levels measurement (NOIR).

9-16   Culture
Reading: Shepard, Chapter 4

9-21   Social Structure
Reading: Shepard, Chapter 5

9-23   Socialization, Part 1
Reading: Shepard, Chapter 6

9-28   Socialization, Part 2

9-30   Groups, Part 1
Reading: Shepard, Chapter 7
(4)   Dr. J's Flea Market
(5)   Practice Test--based on Chapter 1 (Bring a #2 lead pencil.)

10-5   Groups, Part 2
Film: "Classical Creatures" (cc4529) This film is about the making of the STAR WARS series. It is used to understand the concept of the division of labor.

FIGURE III
DETAILED SYLLABUS
(Con't)

(6)   Help Session for Test 1.

(7)   10-7   TEST #1 (based on Chapters 2-7 in Shepard, plus lectures).

Late in the semester I like to hold open office hours (10) during the formal class time. It allows me to get more acquainted with my students particularly in the jumbo classes. Even if your department does not recommend it, I suggest you hold formal office hours (11) during examination week. Students very much appreciate it. And, if no one comes, you can work on next semester's syllabus or lectures. (Someone will come, however).

Lastly, always put your grading scale (12) on your syllabus. Most schools require it and your students will want to know it.

I have tried to show in this section the importance of setting course goals and the place of the syllabus in codifying those goals. Try to avoid any nasty surprises in your course organization. Well thought out course goals and a syllabus representing those goals is a good start. This serves in eliminating bad feelings about sociology and creating a worthwhile intellectual experience for your students.

In the next section, I discuss lecture preparation and the art of lecturing.

REFERENCES

American Sociological Association 1991. *Liberal Learning and the Sociology Major*. Washington, DC.: American Sociological Association.

Wilson, E. K 1990. "A Checklist for Reviewing Syllabi" in K. McKinney and J. Sikora (eds.) *Introductory Sociology Resource Manual*. 3rd edition. Washington DC.: ASA Teaching Resources Center.

SECTION THREE
LECTURE PREPARATION

Introduction

The lecture is the core of any introduction to any sociology course. In this section I discuss how an award winning professor lectures. Following this are some guidelines for preparing lectures. The section concludes with some suggestions for the presentation of lectures.

For the last several years I have been doing research on award winning teachers (Lewis, 1993). Although these teachers come from many disciplines, their views are useful for understanding the lecturing process in introductory sociology.

John Henry Newman (1912) wrote that a professor displays " . . . science in its most complete and winning form, pouring it forth with the zeal of enthusiasm, and lighting up his own love of it in the breast of his hearers." There are many ways this "lighting up" can be achieved in the educational enterprise. Award-winning professors represent a rich font of resources of knowledge and expertise in lighting up undergraduates. Both neophyte teachers and experienced professionals can learn from outstanding teachers. For the past several years I have been doing oral histories of professors who won Kent State University's Distinguished Teaching Award.

Research Procedure

I tape recorded in-depth interviews with the winners of the Alumni Association's Distinguished Teaching Award (DTA) winners. I completed interviews with fifty (50) of the eligible candidates. The interviews were transcribed, and I did a qualitative analysis of material. The interviewing focused on several aspects of undergraduate teaching. First, the professor's social and academic background were described. Second, various aspects of the teaching enterprise were explored including philosophies of teaching and learning and styles of lecturing. Third, techniques of testing and grading used by the professor were investigated. Fourth, the perceptions that the award winning professor had of the joys (and sorrows) of undergraduate teaching were examined. These interviews generated a wealth of material about the craft of teaching in the sciences, social sciences, and humanities.

Styles of Teaching

I could identify five styles of teaching used by the professors interviewed. They are presented in order of importance and are labeled goal-setting, preparation, enthusiasm, humor and performance.

Goal Setting. Award-winning professors clearly have goals in mind when they organize and present their undergraduate courses. These goals are a mixture of the philosophical and pragmatic. They want to both express the excitement of their discipline as well as the core knowledge of the subject particularly in its most up-to-date form. To illustrate, I draw on the comments of three teachers from English, Geology, and Psychology. English Professor: (My goals) " . . . are to teach a sense of order . . . within the enjoyment of what one is reading and the questions that one asks there is an inner order . . . In addition I want to communicate why I am an English major . . . " Geology Professor: "I try to make the student feel that what I was teaching them at that moment was the most important possible thing that they could learn in their entire four years of undergraduate studies." Psychology Professor: "... one major goal that I think of myself trying to accomplish is to challenge everyday misconceptions . . . I view that as perhaps one function of the course and maybe one function of liberal arts."

Preparation. Award-winning teachers spend considerable effort and time on preparation. I became concerned about my own preparation when I learned through the research how much time professors spent getting ready for lectures.

English Professor: (Preparing a lecture on a Shakespeare play), "I'll go over it three or four times and I will write. Then, I'll look at the notes from the critics and see how they fit into my own ideas . . . " Geology Professor: "...The day before I was going to lecture on a particular subject, I would go through my file of overhead projection displays . . . So, I would go through my mental gymnastics of my lecture the second

I have it to the class . . . " Another professor in the sample, a sociologist, said he prepared three times as well: At the start of the semester, at the beginning of the week of the particular class, and on the day of the lecture.

Enthusiasm. This is probably the best known variable associated with good teaching. Both of the groups in the Tollefson and Tracy study ranked it as the most important factor in outstanding teaching. However, my interviews show that enthusiasm is not as one dimensional as it might seem. I found a difference between enthusiasm for the subject and enthusiasm for students. Sometimes students can get in the way of the professor. I had expected the kindly "Mr. Chips." That was clearly not true.

English Professor: "I want to share my enthusiasm. So I take off a mile a minute in the classroom and feel free to digress . . . " Geology Professor: "I try to make the student aware of the fact that . . . regardless of what they are going to do in subsequent life, geology is going to have an impact on them . . . ".

Humor. The factor of humor was important to the teachers. It is discussed in detail in Section Ten.

Performance. Many award-winning professors enjoy the performance aspect of teaching. Some actually report a high from the lecturing experience. When one hears "I would really miss teaching," I think this refers to the entertaining aspects of lecturing. An administrator from another university said it bluntly: "All good teachers are hams."

When I presented this variable at the University of Ulster, it caused a negative reaction. One member of the audience went as far as to ask if teachers should join "The Royal Shakespeare Company." While I do not want professors to go that far, I think they should be sensitive to the performance dimensions of effective lecturing.

Lecture preparation

Let's look at each of these factors as we think about the lectures we are preparing for the introductory course. In relation to **goal-setting**, you should ask yourself a variety of questions about each lecture. First, what are you trying to accomplish that day? How does your lecture fit into the general goals of the course? Again, the importance of thinking through what you want to accomplish in the course, in terms of general goals, reappears. For example, if you are lecturing on the family, what aspects of social structure are you going to deal with? Are you going to deal with kinship or place of religion in effective family decision making? It is essential that you have set some day goals. If you can't think of good reasons (goals) for being in the classroom, why would your students think they should be there?

Preparation is valued by all teachers. No one should go into a lecture knowingly unprepared. But, exactly what does preparation mean? First and foremost, it means you know the subject you are teaching. This monograph focuses on teaching tips, but no matter how creative your teaching is, if you don't know your subject matter, you are in **DEEP TROUBLE**. Sometimes instructors, for whatever reason, are tempted to go into a classroom and wing it. Don't do it. It harms your students because they have paid for the lectures. It also harms you and the profession of sociology because of the lost chance to do quality analytical work.

Second, it is confidence with the material that you are presenting. I found that award winning professors did considerable preparation. In my own case, in a course I have already taught, I review the day's lectures three times. Once before the semester begins, once at the beginning of the week of the lecture and once on the day of the lecture. At the start of the semester, I think through what I am going to say. Next, I decide what I need in terms of supporting materials such as overheads, handouts or books from which I may be quoting. You need to make sure your data presentation are available. On the second review, I make sure all these materials are available. On the day of the lecture, I pack the materials into my briefcase. For a new course, I try not to prepare anything new on the day of the lecture although one is always tempted to do so. After the lecture is presented, I often get ideas for new material suggested by questions from students. I try to make notes on revising the lecture as soon as possible after it is completed using the best questions from my students.

Enthusiasm is a slippery idea to define, but it seems that most good teachers have it and let it show. But, enthusiastic about what? There may be two possibilities. One can be enthusiastic for teaching per se or for the subject one is teaching. When I began my inquiries into the styles of award winning teachers I thought that enthusiasm would be a factor but I was surprised by its location. Most of my interviewees had a great passion for their subjects which they wanted to tell to their students. But, as a group they were not kindly "Mr. Chips" (or "Ms.") who taught merely for the love of teaching. To a person they were frustrated and even angry with students who did not take "their" subject seriously. My advice to you is to let the passion for your sociological imagination show in your lectures. For the most part students will appreciate it.

Almost all of the professors I interviewed said that they used **humor** in one form or another in their lectures. Most of the humor was planned as expected from a group of professors who did as much preparation as these award winning professors did. I have devoted the entirety of Section Ten to the subject of humor and the teaching of sociology.

Performance is a two edged sword. For some professors it is a thrill to teach (perform) in front of students, for others it is frightening to them. But the entertainment quality of teaching is a factor that must be dealt with whether we like it or not. Since students spend a great deal of time and energy watching television and theater films, why would we not expect them to want to be entertained? But, what does performance mean in the teaching context? I believe performance has three components: script, drama and physicality. In one sense the entire lecture is a performance. However, I reserve the idea of performance for any episode occurring in class that has clear beginning and ending. These episodes have a <u>script</u> in the sense that they are planned, have logical order to them, and use the same words and gestures. The telling of a joke is planned at certain times in a lecture. It is logical because it is tied into the content of the lecture or is done for obvious reasons such as reducing tension. Lastly, the words and gestures of the joke are told the same way each time.

The second component of performance is <u>drama</u>. By this I mean that an episode tries to capture the emotions of a sociological idea. When I teach about incest in the family, I read the following from William Shakespeare's ***Hamlet***:

> My father's brother, but no more life my father
> Than I to Hercules: within a month:
> Ere yet the salt of most unrighteous tears
> Had left the flushing in her galled eyes,
> She married. O, most wicked speed to post
> with such dexterity to incestuous sheets!
> > ***Hamlet*** Act I, Scene III.

It shows the passion and drama associated with this social problem.

The last dimension of performance is <u>physicality</u>. Most teachers will knowingly or unknowingly develop gestures as part of episodes they use in their lectures. This can range from simply pointing to a bulletin board to a complex miming of a social situation. My view is that this physicality does not distract from the teaching of sociological ideas. However, you must be comfortable doing it. It might be a good idea to videotape some of your lectures to learn about your use of episodes. Or, if this is not possible, have a colleague evaluate your teaching focusing only on the use of the episode in his or her observations.

I express my performances in four ways. First, I do short imaginary exchanges with fictional characters. One of them is "Martha" my wife; another is "a student from Ashtabula" who is naive, [Ashtabula is a small town in northeast Ohio]; and third is a bright student who knows the answer to a question I have posed. I use the skit between my characters and me to make a point for the class and, for me, that performance has more impact than the usual lecture. For example, Martha is with me when I talk about private and public space. I make a comment on it noting the actions that a young couple is putting on. I (JML) say, "See that couple over by the coke machine - they are fighting but they don't want others to get involved". Martha: "How do you know?" JML: "Because . . ." and then I explain to Martha the sociological idea of civil inattention. Martha will also chastise me if she thinks the joke I told is off color. These fictional characters have a personality of their own that students can identify with over the semester.

Second, I play games with students. For example, when I teach Eric Erickson's eight stages of socialization, I play a game of softball catch with students in the class. So, during class, I will play roles from an infant to an elderly person playing catch. The students do seem to remember Erickson's stages.

Third, I tell jokes. The stories are related to the material of the lecture. For example, to illustrate the concept of "the definition of the situation" or differential perceptions, I tell the story of Matilda, an 85 year old woman who goes to her physician who, after an examination, informs her that she is pregnant. "But, Doctor, I'm eighty-five years old". The doctor says, "I know, but you're pregnant". She decides to call her husband, Fred, who is 89. He picks up the phone hearing Matilda saying excitedly, "Fred, I'm pregnant!" Fred replies, "Who is this?"

I must admit that I enjoy the fact that I have made over 60 or 600 people laugh. I worry that too much humor gets in the way of the lecture and the students, while laughing, are not learning. I think the students appreciate these activities. My qualitative course evaluations show this. What does worry me is that my colleagues both in and out of sociology will judge my teaching as frivolous. And, that is the other edge of this sword. That is, too much theater may create a situation where you are not seen as a serious person, which is the death knell for a scholar. Fourth, I do role plays. Generally they are planned but sometimes they are spontaneous. For example, I use a planned role play in teaching particularly labeling theory. I will play a student who rarely comes to class asking a good student to lend me his or her class notes for a weekend. It is very interesting to see how the good student responds often labeling the poor student as a deviant for not going to class. Typically I ask for volunteers offering them a prize of a candy bar to participate.

An example of a spontaneous role play occurred once when I was teaching about the exchange theory and the sharing of class notes. It hit me to do a role play of a student who does not go to class asking a good student who does for notes. The role-play worked and I now do it regularly in my classes.

All four of these types are performances because they are episodes having a script, drama and physicality. My recommendation is that you are probably doing it right now and you should build on your successes to make your lecture as interesting and productive as possible.

The Accouterments to Lecturing

Here I discuss three things you can do to support your lecturing in the introductory course. They are discussion questions, handouts and visual materials.

Discussion Questions

Discussion questions are very useful for getting students thinking about the subject under consideration. You can use the questions that are in the instructor's manuals that come with most textbooks packages or you can develop your own.

The essential thing about discussion questions is that students must be given a chance to think about them. We cannot assume that students can formulate a response as rapidly as we could do it. Some professors provide a list of discussion questions for the entire quarter or semester, but these have a way of getting lost. I think it is better to link them to logical categories such as theory, methods and social institutions giving them out when you reach these topics. Discussion questions can be used in a variety of ways. First, they can be openers for raising sociological questions. You might ask the day before the lectures on family: "Discuss the influence of your family on your decision to attend (college or university). Did any particular member of your family have more influence on you than other members? Why is this case?" You could ask your students to be prepared to respond to these questions at the opening of class. Sometimes a surprising category of relative comes up in the second question and this can lead to interesting discussion. A second way is at the end of a lecture you can break students into "buzz" groups and have them deal with a question related to the lecture. I have had good luck with this question after a presentation on Weber's thesis: "Do you see any relationship between your religion and your work?" "Do religious values influence your work values?" I have used this question in large sections getting feedback by having students applaud their answers to the follow up question i.e., "How many of you are influenced by religion in your work?" It is essential that you develop ways to allow students to share their discussions with you and the class members. One way to do it is to have each buzz group elect a reporter who summarizes the results of the question. I have sometimes used newsprint on the wall with the summaries written there. This does not work very well for classes above fifty students. The verbal summary does work for larger classes.

Discussion questions are also useful ways for students to prepare for examinations if you use essay type questions. Students like to have clear expectations of what is going to be on the examination (actually they would like to have the examination). Discussion questions can provide a basis for preparing essay examinations. If you tell your students that the essay questions are derived from discussion questions then you have a higher chance of them preparing when the question is to be discussed. I am sure you can come up with many other ways to use discussion questions. Don't be discouraged if they do not work the first time. They will, eventually. In the next section are core lectures that may be useful to you in developing your Introduction to Sociology course. Each lecture has a few discussion questions with it.

Joseph Janes and Diana Hauer (1988: 47) suggest that there are several types of discussion questions including one type they label "higher order questions" which calls for abstract thinking by students. Janes and Hauer (1988: 47-49) identify six functions for learning higher order questions. First, there is **evaluation** which calls for judgment, value and choice. For example, when presenting types of data collection methods, you might ask your students to evaluate whether surveys or participant observation would be the best way to collect attitudinal data on the homeless. Second, there are **inference** questions which call for deductive or inductive reasoning. Many introductory textbooks have sections on how to reason. To help your students develop critical thinking skills you might ask them, for example, to make deductive inferences from a general theory of power to specific hypotheses about power relationships between men and women. Third, there are **comparative** questions which ask if ideas or objects are " . . . similar, dissimilar, unrelated or contradictory" (Janes and Hauer, 1988, p. 48). When asking about levels of measurement (See Hoover handout, P. 29) you might ask if measuring attitudes is similar to measuring behavior - I think it is, but we might want to debate this. Nevertheless, a comparative question is warranted.

Fourth are **application** questions. Again, concerning levels of measurement, we might ask our students if the question, "From Monday to Thursday, I study every night, 3 nights a week, two nights a week, one night a week or none", is a nominal, ordinal or interval variable. Fifth are **problem solving** questions that lead the student to see the relationship between previous learned knowledge and some problem. For example, the student might be asked what type of measure of variation would he or she use with the means derived from frequencies of time spent studying. Sixth, are **cause and effect** questions. While these are more typical in the physical sciences, they can be asked in beginning sociology. In explaining correlations (and some introductory textbooks have begun to introduce this statistic) you can use cause and effect questions to point out why cause and correlation is different. One of my colleagues asks his students, using the old game show *Name That Tune*, to name the song, "Correlation is not ____" Of course, the answer is causation.

Janes and Hauer (1988: p. 49) write that higher order discussion questions: "Imaginative use of higher questions can enliven an otherwise dull classroom discussion".

Handouts

Handouts fall into two categories - those taken from secondary sources and those that you develop yourself. Typically handouts serve as surrogates for material that you do not want to put on a blackboard or read to your students. Handouts are either data or some sort of classification system or typology. With secondary handouts you need to be careful not to violate copyright regulations of fair usage. Of course, this is not a problem with your own material.

There are two basic rules for handout preparation. First, as with journal article tables, the handout should stand alone. That is, the students should have all the information on the handout to use it. Second, the student should have a clear understanding why she or he is getting the handout. I like to put a discussion question or two on each handout I give to my sociology "Intro" students.

A new issue about handouts has developed in recent years. Some departments are beginning to put restrictions on the number of copies because of cost. I have known of some departments that charge students for handouts - the "pay as you go" plan, (I hope no chair reads this). Figure IV is a handout taken from Hoover (1984) that I use early in the course when discussing measurement.

FIGURE IV
SECONDARY SOURCE HANDOUT

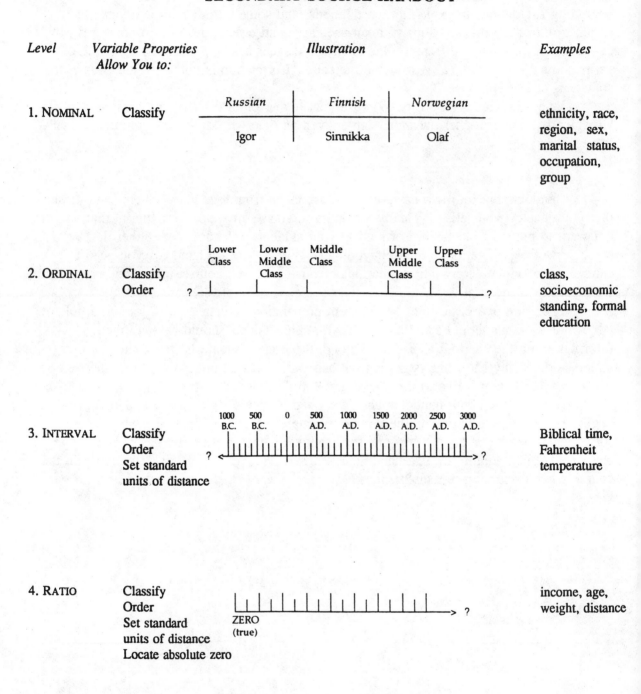

Level	Variable Properties Allow You to:	Illustration	Examples
1. NOMINAL	Classify	Russian | Finnish | Norwegian Igor | Sinnikka | Olaf	ethnicity, race, region, sex, marital status, occupation, group
2. ORDINAL	Classify Order	Lower Class, Lower Middle Class, Middle Class, Upper Middle Class, Upper Class	class, socioeconomic standing, formal education
3. INTERVAL	Classify Order Set standard units of distance	1000 B.C. 500 B.C. 0 500 A.D. 1000 A.D. 1500 A.D. 2000 A.D. 2500 A.D. 3000 A.D.	Biblical time, Fahrenheit temperature
4. RATIO	Classify Order Set standard units of distance Locate absolute zero	ZERO (true)	income, age, weight, distance

Here are some discussion questions that I link to this handout either in a transparency or directly in a handout.

1.   Which of these measures is the most scientific? the least? Why?

2.   Which of these levels of measurement is the most difficult to obtain? Why? The easiest?

3.   The box on page _____ of your text uses what type of measure?

4.   How would you create an ordinal measure from a nominal measure?

Figure V is a handout that is original and involves the administrative aspects of the course.

FIGURE V
AN ORIGINAL HANDOUT

INTRODUCTION TO SOCIOLOGY
SPRING SEMESTER, 1994

STAFF/OFFICE HOURS

1. **JERRY M. LEWIS**, Professor of Sociology. Professor Lewis received his B.A. from Cornell College, M.S. from Boston University and his Ph.D. from the University of Illinois. He has been a member of the Kent State University faculty since 1966. His research interests are in the area of crowd behavior, particularly soccer crowds. Office Hours: Monday: 5-7 P.M.; Tuesday and Thursday: 8:30 to 10 A.M. in 140 Lowry.

2. **HARRIET MARTINEAU**, Doctoral Assistant. Harriet lives in Ravenna. Her research interests deal with formal organizations. Office hours: Tuesday, 12 to 3 in the Soc Lab.

3. **EMILE DURKHEIM**, Graduate Assistant. Emile is from Buffalo and lives in Kent. His research looks at deviance. Office Hours: Wednesday, 12-3 in the Soc Lab.

4. **MAX WEBER**, Graduate Assistant. Max studied at Heidelberg University. He lives in Kent. His research examines religion. He is in charge of the help sessions.

5. **JANELL LEWIS**, Undergraduate Assistant. Janell is a Sociology major. She lives in Kent. Her research interests are in theory and gender. Office Hours: Thursday, 12-2 in the Soc Lab.

7. **SOCIOLOGY LAB**: It is open from 9:00-3:00 P.M. on Tuesday, Wednesday and Thursday in 143 Lowry Hall. You may get help from any graduate assistant who is there or from the staff of the course.

When you telephone my office (672-2708), please give your name and have your ID ready. We are happy to talk with you about sociology. However, grades are NEVER given over the telephone.

Visual Materials

There is an enormous amount of material available to the "Intro" teacher including transparencies, television, films and movies. One has to choose carefully what she or he wants to use. In evaluating this material, I think the instructor should ask three questions:

1. Does the material help the student understand the sociological concept under consideration?

2. How will I evaluate the student's knowledge of these materials?

3. Can these materials be efficiently used in the classroom?

Let's look at each of these questions.

Does the material help the student understand the sociological material under consideration?

We may think that our visual material is a terrific illustration of a particular idea, but we may have assumed too much about our students' background. One textbook I used has a picture of the Kennedy family (JFK, RFK). I tried to initiate a discussion about this picture and what it meant to the understanding of the power elite. I found out that my students knew very little about the family and particularly the background of how Joseph Kennedy came to power. So you need to be careful about what you want to accomplish with the visual material. As a model, use the politician's model of KISS - Keep it simple, stupid. Or, ASSUME - If you assume too much you make an "ass" out of "U" and "me".

Am I able to evaluate the student's knowledge of the visual material?

You may find a film that illustrates what you are trying to teach. However, it may take twenty to thirty minutes to show the film and a few scenes are about what you want to accomplish. You end asking one or two multiple choice questions or one essay question for thirty minutes of classroom activity. You may think that it is worth it, or you may not be concerned about evaluation at all. But, it is a decision you have to make because your students will want to know your expectations for them in terms of their learning and testing.

I try to solve the evaluation problem by developing materials that speak to several sociological issues. For example, I show a film called "Principles of Caste" (1980) which illustrates the stratification of religion and work on family life. Then, I can ask several questions related to the film.

Can the materials be efficiently presented to students?

Here I am concerned about the mechanics of presentation of overhead transparencies, television films and theater movies.

Transparencies

Are transparencies easy to prepare? Is there an overhead in the classroom? Can students see it? There are two kinds of transparencies (overheads).

The first are those that you make and second are ones that textbook publishers provide. Most departments can make overheads although they are likely to be in black and white. Publisher's transparencies are usually, but not always, in color. If your college or university has an audiovisual department, it probably can create color overheads. You should receive a set of transparency masters or the actual transparencies when you adopt a book. It has been my experience that they are very well produced. Typically, there are three content categories in any set. The first these deal with is social theory. For example, a transparency can show the linkage between culture and social structure. Second, there are typologies for classifying social patterns. Most transparency sets will have the Merton anomie typology in it. Third, transparencies will have data displays ranging from occupational prestige rankings to world population patterns. Some transparencies are based on census data. When showing them, you can talk about how sociologists use census data.

Television programs and theater films

Television films and movies require considerable effort to present. You should have the equipment readily available and it must work. There is nothing more frustrating than to have a movie projector breakdown during the showing of the film. I suggest you develop a solid working knowledge of VCR's and movie projectors. Let's now talk about specific forms of the visual materials.

There are three sources of television films. Those that are available from film services, those created for introductory courses and those that you copy from broadcasts. It is probably better to use ones that come from film services or that are ancillaries with the text you adopt since copyright and fair usage criteria have been met by the distributors. However, you may see television programs that are germane to your course. News programs, public broadcasting and news magazine shows such as ABC's *20/20* all provide materials that are useful for teaching the introductory course. I have a colleague who teaches the sociology sport who tells me that he could not teach it if he did not copy and use television programs. There is so much material available to the instructor. However, the criteria proposed at the start of this chapter should be considered when deciding whether to use television sources in your lectures.

In closing this section of **TIPSTEACH,** I want to address a question that I am often asked when I talk about teaching the introductory course - "How long does it take you to prepare a new lecture?" I asked the same question in my study of distinguished teachers and got a range of answers including "a lifetime." In responding to the question, I am drawing on my own experience and the answer is roughly two to three work days depending on your familiarity with the material. This translates into three to four months of work, so, if possible, give yourself plenty of time when preparing your first introductory course. Now that I have created a panic in terms
of lecture preparation, let me offer you some help. The next section lays out nine lecture outlines for core lectures in introductory sociology courses.

REFERENCES

Hoover, K. R. 1988. *The Elements of Social Scientific Thinking*. Fourth Edition. New York: St. Martin's Press.

Janes, J. and Hauer, D. 1988. *NOW WHAT readings on surviving (and even enjoying) your experience at college teaching*. Second Edition. Littleton, Mass.: Copley Publishing Group.

Lewis, J. 1993. "Teaching Style of Award-winning Professors" in R. Ellis, (ed.) *Quality Assurance for University Teaching*. Bristol, England: Open University: 149-164.

Newman, J. H. (Cardinal) 1912. *The Idea of A University*. Notre Dame, IN: University of Notre Dame Press.

SECTION FOUR
CORE LECTURE OUTLINES

This section presents nine core lecture outlines that may be useful to you as you begin developing your introductory course. By core lectures, I mean presentations that usually are made in most introductory courses. The lectures have either been developed for this monograph or are modifications of lectures I designed for instructor's manuals. The first three lectures usually are presented early in the course. Lectures Four through Eight are given in the middle of the course. The last one is usually positioned at the end of the course. Although these outlines are detailed, they should be seen as a starting point as you begin to build your course and not as substitutes for your own hard work. You will likely want to modify these considerably to fit the needs of your students as well as your own scholarly concerns.

Lectures and the Student Cultures

Any Introduction to Sociology lectures should draw on the student cultures for illustrations of sociological ideas. There are many student cultures in a college or university. There is, of course, the culture of the classroom which is rich in material for sociological illustrations (Bricher, 1992). But, there are others not directly tied to the classroom. It seems to me that there are five student cultures at most colleges or universities. Some students, particularly freshmen in an introductory course, may not be aware of these cultures. "Intro" can make students aware of these cultures as well as suggesting ways to interpret their experiences with them. These cultures include film, sports spectator, sports participation, concert, and the intellectual-non class related.

Film culture

There are many films offered each year on campuses at low prices. The films are shown in college or university facilities easily reached by students. I did an analysis of films shown at Kent State University for 1990-1991 and the findings were impressive.

In the academic year 1990-1991 there were 35 films shown Friday and Saturday nights at an admission price of $1.50. The range of films was from *War of the Roses* to *Dances with Wolves*. In addition to *Dances with Wolves* there were other award-winning films such as *Born on the Fourth of July*, *Driving Miss Daisy*, *My Left Foot*, *Dick Tracy*, and *Ghost*. There were several important international films shown on Kent's campus in 1990-1991 including *Henry V*, *Cinema Paradiso*, *The Seventh Seal*, and *Potemkin*.

Most films present some grist for the sociological mill. *Born on the Fourth of July*, starring Tom Cruise, could be used in the culture or deviance sections of the introductory course as an illustration of how groups within society treated the disabled. Or, parts of it could be shown concerning collective behavior and social movements as an illustration of an anti-Vietnam war rally. Martin Tolich (1992) writes that showing all or parts of films in class, ". . . provides students with the opportunity to see meat on the bare bones of sociological analysis." If you don't want to send your students to watch the films in a realistic theater setting, renting the film is a possibility. Because they are being shown in a nonprofit setting, they fall under the fair usage provisions of the copyright rules.

Sports spectator

In many colleges and universities, students, through fees, "pay" for all their tickets to sporting events. They are admitted to all sporting events without further charge with a valid ID. However, this is not true for the large football and basketball powers. The obvious sports that should generate a strong undergraduate presence are football and men's basketball. Teachers of Introductory Sociology should follow the activities of their schools' teams and comment on them as appropriate. One way to do this is by analyzing the deviant stereotypes that develop regarding student athletes (see Lecture Six). Many schools, while not having success in "major" sports, do well in the "minor" ones such as volleyball, field hockey, wrestling or track. Students should be informed that going to these programs costs very little, if anything.

Sport Participation Culture

Nowadays, most schools have intramural facilities that get active use through competitive programs, workout circuits and three season walking trails. The participation fees for students in most of these programs (walking is free) are nominal. Following the exploits of your students in these competitions can be very interesting. You often use intramural activities to illustrate social organization and leadership ideas. For example, you might explore with your students what type of leadership structure is best for a successful intramural team.

Concert Culture

Over the course of the academic year, there is a wide range of campus concerts, plays and other performances that are presented to students at low cost. Often rock concerts are well attended and this is understandable. You might want to tie these concerts into a lecture on popular culture.

Intellectual - non class related

Departments, colleges and the university all have programs where outside speakers talk on a wide range of subjects. The introductory teacher should encourage students to attend these lectures encouraging the value that students can learn something without expecting a "grade" or some reward. However, having said this, these programs do lend themselves to extra credit assignments. (Yes, I am not always idealistic). For example, in the Spring of 1993, Richard Gelles, an expert on family violence, spoke eloquently at Kent State. Some of my students heard his lecture because of an extra credit assignment.

THE FIRST DAY

The first day of class is very important. Lecture One gives you some guidelines for it.

LECTURE 1 - THE FIRST CLASS

I.   **Rationale**

The first day is very important. There are a variety of things you can do to make it a good experience for you and your students. You need to be well organized.

II.   **Before the first class**

If you are not familiar with the classroom, I suggest you visit it to check for problems such as enough seats and if the audio-visual equipment is in order. Make sure you have enough copies of the syllabi and that any overheads you plan to use are completed. (I like to have an overhead saying "Welcome to Sociology 12050" "Professor J. M. Lewis").

III.   **The day of first class**

On the first day of class, arrive early, as there likely will be students waiting who need to ask you questions.

A.   Hand out three by five cards to get pertinent information from students. If your department does not have a form for this, I recommend the following: name, campus (or other) address, and telephone number, proposed major, father's and mother's occupation, and hometown.

B.   After this is completed, have students get telephone numbers from at least two other students. (This will save you time and is a mini-icebreaker).

C.   Hand out the syllabus and go over it carefully. The major things to point out in your review are the reading assignments, the examinations and the project due dates.

IV.   **The Opening Lecture**

This is crucial. I do not think that you should dismiss your class early as it sends a message that you do not have anything to do because you are not prepared. The lecture should have both didactic and inspirational components.

A.   Didactic components

This part of the lecture reviews the elements of theoretical thinking.

1.   Model
2.   Theory
3.   Concept
4.   Proposition
5.   Hypothesis
6.   Variable

B. Inspirational components

1.   How sociology fits in the liberal arts curriculum.
2.   What students can expect to get out of the course.
3   Your interest in sociology including your own research.

V.   **Resources**

Dorn, D. S. "The First Day of Class: Problems and Strategies."
Teaching Sociology. 15: 61-72 (1987)

Rifer, R. L. "The First Class." *Teaching Sociology*. 10: 262-265
(1983)
Wallace, W. L. "Toward a Disciplinary Matrix in Sociology". in N. J.
Smelser (ed.), *Handbook of Sociology*.
Newbury Park, CA: Sage., (1988), Chapter One.

SOCIAL THEORY

Almost all beginning courses start with an overview of theory. In many ways, this is because the textbooks used in the introductory course begin with the theory. As noted earlier, most textbooks divide theory into the "Big Three" of structural-functionalism, conflict and symbolic interactionism. Here are two lecture outlines that should help you get started on structural-functionalism and symbolic interactionism lectures.

LECTURE 2 - THE SOCIOLOGY OF EMILE DURKHEIM

I.   **Rationale**

Most sociologists think that the scholarship of Emile Durkheim was crucial to the discipline development. A general overview lecture on Durkheim would help students understand the place of his theory in sociological inquiry particularly structural-functionalism.

II.   **Review Structural-functional theory**

Begin your lecture by reviewing some of the basic ideas of structural-functionalism including equilibrium, system, manifest and latent functions.

III.   **Durkheim's background**

A. Demographics

1. Born: 1855; died:1917.
2. French.
3. Son of rabbi.
4. Educated at the Ecole Normale Superieure in Paris.

B. Impact on French Sociology

IV.   **Major works**

A.   *The Division of Labor in Society* (1893)
B.   *The Rules of Sociological Method* (1895)
C.   *Suicide* (1897)
D.   *The Elementary Forms of the Religious Life* (1912)

V.   **Basic concepts**

A.   Social facts (chose)

1.   Constraint
2.   Exteriority

B.   Collective Conscience

C.   Types of suicide

1.   Egoistic
2.   Altruistic
3.   Anomie
4.   Fatalistic

VI.   **Central propositions**

A.   Society sets probabilities for suicide. **Comment:** Your lecture should develop the idea that society shapes the chances for suicide using Durkheim's four types: egoistic, altruistic, anomie, and fatalism.
B.   Suicide rates are social facts. **Comment:** You should stress suicide rates remain constant suggesting that these rates meet the definition of a social fact. That is, the rates can only be explained by other social facts.

At this point, you can bring in C. Wright Mills' idea about the sociological imagination investigating a social problem by linking it to social structure.

VII. **Application**

    A.   An interesting application of Durkheim's ideas is to look at risk taking behavior of young men in American culture using the debate over motorcycle riders and helmet use at this point.

VIII. **Application discussion questions**

    A.   What social facts encourage young males in American society into taking greater physical risks than others?

    B.   Why do some male bike riders consider wearing a helmet unmanly?

IX. **Resources**

Jones, Robert A., *Emile Durkheim*, Beverly Hills: Sage, 1986.

Turner, Jonathan H., Leonard Beeghley, Charles H. Powers, The *Emergence of Sociological Theory*, Edition, Belmont CA: Wadsworth, 1989.

LECTURE 3 - **DRAMATURGICAL THEORY**

I.   **Rationale**

Students are not always comfortable with the idea that social interaction can be understood as theater. A useful way to teach Goffman's dramaturgical model is by applying it to a theater film.

II.   **Review of Symbolic Interactionism**

Begin your lecture by reviewing some of the basic ideas of symbolic interaction including self, symbol and subjective interpretations.

III.   **Review of Dramaturgical theory**

A review of E. Goffman's theory should include impression management teams and audiences, adornments, performances, props and front and back regions.

IV.   *Tootsie*.

Next, show some or all of the film *Tootsie* (1982) to your students. If you are unable to do this you might make overheads from film reviews.

A.   Film synopsis: Dustin Hoffman as Michael and "Tootsie" is an out-of-work actor who gets a part on a soap opera by dressing as an older women. His character becomes a hit. He further complicates his situation by falling in love with one of the female stars of the soap, played by Jessica Lange. In turn, her father, played by Charles Durning, falls in love with "Tootsie".

V.   **Analysis**

A.   Impression management: Michael as Dorothy (Tootsie) trying to convince people and generally succeeding that he is a middle-aged woman.

B.   Teams and Audiences: Tootsie acts in a team performance with his roommate played by Bill Murray. There are many audiences including the TV audience as well as the cast of the soap. In addition the characters played by Charles Durning, Terry Garr (as Michael's girl friend) also serve as audiences.

C.   Adornment: This happens when Michael becomes Dorothy (Tootsie).

D.   Props: "Tootsie's" purse.

E.   Regions, front and back: Michael, as he prepares to be Dorothy, is in a back region. As Dorothy, he is in "her" front region. Some of the great humor of the film comes from the back and front region confusion.

VI.   **Resources**

E. Goffman, *The Presentation of Self in Everyday Life*. Garden City, New
    York; Doubleday and Company, 1959.

METHODS

After theory comes methods, which I have always had a tough time teaching because I feel I never give the subject enough time. However, one should not turn the introductory course into a dissertation on methods. The first thing I like to do is give students a "sense of measurement." This can be done with lecture on this topic entitled, "Levels of Measurement." This is followed by one on designing a survey. This outline is presented below. Depending on the amount of class participation you are able to generate, this lecture may develop into two lectures.

LECTURE 4 - DEVELOPING THE SURVEY QUESTIONNAIRE

I.   Rationale

The rationale for this lecture is to develop an appreciation of the place of the survey in sociological inquiry. It is designed to develop critical skills in evaluating questionnaires used in face-to-face, telephone or mail surveys.

II.   Theory

Students need to understand how operational definitions are derived from theories. Most introductory textbooks have sections that you can build on in your lecture.

III.   Face-to-face, telephone and mailed surveys

Here you provide your students with a general overview of the different types of data collecting procedures. Usually you can build on the textbook's presentation of this material.

IV.   Survey questions

Understanding the logic behind survey questions is the central point of this part of the lecture. The key to a successful discussion of question is to have many examples. You might even hand out a completed questionnaire as you make the presentation.

        A.   Levels of measurement (See handout p. 28 and refer to the lecture on level of measurement)

                1.   Nominal
                2.   Ordinal
                3.   Interval
                4.   Ratio

        B.   Types of Questions

                1.   Demographic

           2.   Attitude
           3.   Behavioral
           4.   Behavioral Intent

    C.   Forms of questions

           1.   Open-ended
           2.   Closed-ended

V.   Sampling

In your presentation, spend time on the idea of random sampling as opposed to purposive sampling.

    A.   Simple random sampling

    B.   Stratified sampling

    C.   Alternatives to random sampling

VI.   The place of interviewing in the social survey

This section allows students to get into the dynamics of the data collecting process. I would encourage as much role-playing and group discussion as possible.

    A.   Techniques for establishing rapport

    B.   Reasons for asking questions as written

    C.   Recording answers

VII.   Ethics of research

This lecture(s) on survey research is a good time to raise ethical issues associated with this type of data collection. Unfortunately, this subject is not always adequately treated in introductory textbooks.

    A.   Working with human subjects review

    B.   Voluntary participation of subjects

    C.   Prevention of subject harm

VIII.   **Application**

Using polls printed in newspapers is a good way to get your student thinking about survey data. If you can't find a poll in a newspaper, *Social Problems* or *Public Opinion Quarterly* are good sources. Encourage your students to write alternative questions to ones in the polls. A nice way to conclude this application is with a buzz group discussion of issues of related reliability and validity. For example, How carefully written are the poll questions? What do you think the poll questions are measuring? How well have the poll questions measured it?

IX.   **Resources**

Babbie, Earl, *The Practice of Social Research*. Fifth   Edition, Belmont, California: Wadsworth, 1989.

Rossi, Peter H., "On Sociological Data" in N. J. Smelser, (ed.) *Handbook of Sociology*. Newbury Park, California: Sage, 1988.

CULTURE AND SOCIAL STRUCTURE

After theory and methods are completed, courses generally turn to issues of culture and social structure. The next lecture builds on these topics by looking at subcultures within society.

LECTURE 5 - UNDERSTANDING SUBCULTURES

I.   **Rationale**

This lecture is designed to help the student understand the place of subcultures within a larger cultural and social context. This basis for the lecture is the cultural organization of graffiti artists. It is based primarily on Brewer and Miller, 1990, as well as my experience with graffiti and soccer hooligans in England.

II.   **Theory**

I think the lecture should link the subculture to society. It is a group that is part of the dominant culture but differs from it in important and clearly distinguishable ways. These ways include demographics, social organization and values. A good way to understand this is to look at the subculture of urban graffiti writers.

III.   **Demographics of graffiti writers**

Here you present a description of the graffiti writers.

      A.   Young (12-22)

      B.   Male

      C.   Inner city residents

      D.   Ethnic background

            1.   Black
            2.   Latino

      E.   Lower and working class, with few middle class artists.

IV.   **Types of graffiti**

Brewer and Miller have developed a classification of the art of graffiti. You want your students to understand that becoming part of a graffiti gang requires learning the rules of drawing as well as the gang's social organizations (next section). You should get slides or overheads of graffiti to illustrate this part of lecture.

      A.   Tags: Stylized signatures in spray paint.

      B.   Throwups: Elaborated names in bubbles or blocks using spray paint.

      C.   Pieces (derived from masterpieces) multi-colored murals.

V.   **Social organization of graffiti writers**

Graffiti writers are part of gangs. This suggests that the gangs have a system of values and norms to follow that may be different from the general society.

      A.   Hierarchy of prestige of drawers

            1.   Elite writers
            2.   Taggers

      B.   Crews (teams)

      C.   Networks

D.   Mentor-Protege relationships

VI.   Value systems

This is a development of the themes suggested in Part V.

A.   Fame

B.   Artistic Expression

C.   Power

D.   Rebellion

VII.   Application

Graffiti seems to be present on every college campus. Ask your students to bring in samples of graffiti. Here are some discussion questions:

A.   Do graffiti writers on campus meet the criteria of being a subculture? Why? Why not?

B.   How would a sociologist interpret the graffiti subculture from a structural-functional, conflict or interactionist perspective?

C.   Do categories of graffiti content vary from one campus to another? Is it possible to classify the graffiti content in terms of erotic and non-erotic content? Political and non-political content?

VIII.   Resources

Brewer, D. and M. L. Miller, "Bombing and Burning: The Social Organization and Values of Hip Hop Graffiti and Implications for Policy". *Deviant Behavior*, pp. 345-369, 1990.

Lachmann, R., "Graffiti as Career and Ideology" *American Journal of Sociology*, 94 (2): 229-250, 1988.

SOCIAL PROCESSES

From culture and social structure the introductory course generally moves to social processes including socialization, deviance, and stratification. Lecture Six combines elements of all three social processes with a focus on the stereotyping of athletes.

LECTURE 6 - STEREOTYPING

I.   Rationale

The purpose of this lecture is to illustrate the social process of stereotyping to your students by showing how varsity athletes become stereotyped.

II.   Review the basic concepts

You should review the basics concepts particularly the differences between prejudice and discrimination.

>   A.   Prejudice
>
>   B.   Discrimination
>
>   C.   Stereotyping

III.   Review some key stereotypes about athletes

Students will have no trouble coming up with stereotypes about athletes.

>   A.   "Dumb jock": Unable to do academic work.
>
>   B.   "Privileged characters": Receives special privileges.
>
>   C.   "Four (five) years and out": The college athlete never graduates.
>
>   D.   "Athletes are not serious people": Athletes are too involved in their sports to be taken seriously.

IV.   Consequences for athletes and the campus community of stereotyping

Stereotypes have consequences for a variety of groups within the community. They can lead to prejudice and discrimination.

>   A.   Prejudice towards athletes.
>
>   B.   Discrimination against athletes.

V. **Data to contradict the stereotypes**

These data refer to Division I athletes, but could be used to stereotype at any level of competition.

  A. "Dumb jock": One study at the University of Minnesota indicated that there was no difference in grade point average between athletes and nonathletes (Leonard, p. 214). However, another study of football players indicated that the mean grade point average was less than 2.00 (Leonard, p. 214). Students should be asked to discuss these findings.

  B. "Privileged characters": It is true that athletes, particularly in Division I, do get some advantages such as early registration. This is true because of the amount of time spent practicing and travelling. These advantages must be placed in a time-demands context.

  C. "Never graduated": This is probably the biggest single stereotype. Male athletes have graduation rates equal to or greater than non-athletes in Division I schools except for football and basketball athletes. (Chronicle, March 27, 1991)

  D. "Serious persons": Athletes have tremendous time demands on them. The successful management of time does suggest that athletes are serious people.

VI. **Application**

Develop a case history of an athlete who has been stereotyped. Perhaps it could be one of your own students or a friend of one of your students. Ask them to share their experiences with your class. Here are some application discussion questions:

  A. Are certain athletes in some sports targets for stereotyping more than those in other sports?

  B. Does the gender of the athlete influence the stereotyping process?

  C. How can the stereotyping processes be changed?

VII.   **Resources**

Leonard II, W. R., *A Sociological Perspective of Sport*, New York: Macmillian, 1984.

"Graduation Rates of Athletes and other Students at Division I Colleges", *The Chronicle of Higher Education*, March 27, 1991. pp. A39-A44.

SOCIAL INSTITUTIONS

A large part of the introductory course is devoted to social institutions typically focusing on the universal institutions of family, education, economy, polity and religion. Lecture outlines seven and eight are for the family and religion.

LECTURE 7 - THE FUTURE FAMILY

I.   **Rationale**

This lecture looks at the future family in the 21st century.

II.   **Theory**

A.   Review the structural-functionalist perspective family

B.   Review of conflict approach to family

III.   **Future trends In the United States**

A.   Increase in alternative family forms

1.   Single parent families
2.   Gay and lesbian marriages
3.   Increases in cohabitation before marriage
4.   Commuter marriages

B.   Increase in two parents working

C.   Continuing high divorce rate

D.   Decline of the "squeaky" clean American family

IV.　Analysis

Interpret the trends developed in part III, comparing and contrasting the structural-functional and conflict perspectives.　Handouts or overheads should be developed to support the analysis.　One of the best resources for looking at the future family is still Bernard Farber's chapter seven in his book *Family*, 1964.

V.　Application

Have students write down the various family forms they have seen in popular culture portrayals on television.

Discussion questions:
- A.　Are alternative forms portrayed on television?
- B.　What functions of the family are developed in television family sitcoms?

VI.　Resources

Farber, B. *Family: Organizations and Interaction*.
San Francisco: Chandler, 1964.

Huber, J. and G. Spitze, "Trends in Family Sociology" in N. J. Smelser (ed.), *Handbook of Sociology*. Newbury Park, CA: Sage, 1988, Chapter 13.

Lecture 8 - SOCIOLOGY OF RELIGIOUS RITUAL

I.　Rationale

This lecture is designed to demonstrate how the religious institution shape people's lives.　The organizing theory is E. Durkheim's analysis of religious ritual.

II.　Theory

A good way to begin is to define religion and then discuss the components of his definition.　Durkheim defines religion as, "A religion is a unified system of beliefs and practices relative to sacred things."

III.　Religious ritual

Begin by describing a religious ritual to your students.　The Roman Catholic mass; A Christmas hymn sung at a Methodist church; or a Jewish Yom Kippur service might be appropriate events.

IV.   **Durkheim's social functions of religion** (after Alpert, 1961)

The next step is to analyze one of the rituals you described using Durkheim's ideas.

       A.   Discipline and preparation function: "Ritual prepares an individual for social living by imposing on him ...self-discipline" (Alpert, p.199).

       B.   Cohesive function: "Ceremony brings people together and thus serves to reaffirm their common   bonds...(Alpert, p. 200).

       C.   Revitalizing function: Rituals help perpetuate and renew the social heritage of the group.

       D.   Euphoric function: Rituals encourage the development of social joy.

V.   **Secular rituals**

You might conclude the lecture with an application of Durkheim's analysis to the study of the functions of secular rituals such as:

       A.   The World Series of Baseball.

       B.   Professional football's Super Bowl.

       C.   The movie industry's Oscar awards.

       D.   Here are some application discussion questions:
           1.   Does the Super Bowl have elements of the four functions of ritual?

           2.   Can a secular ritual serve as an alternative to religious ritual?

VI.   **Resources**

Alpert, H, *Emile Durkheim and his Sociology*, New York: Russell and Russell, 1961.

Durkheim, E., *The Elementary Forms of the Religious Life*, trans: J. W. Swain, New York: Collier Books, 1961 (1915).

Wuthnow, R. J., "Sociology of Religion", in N. J. Smelser, ed., *Handbook of Sociology*, Newbury Park: Sage, 1988.

SOCIAL CHANGE

Social change, while a process, is often dealt with at the end of the introductory course. Sociologists focus on collective behavior, social movements, broad societal change and urban change. Lecture outline nine suggests a way to investigate the sociology of crowds.

LECTURE 9 - **THE SOCIOLOGY OF CROWDS**

I.   **Rationale**

The purpose of this lecture is to encourage your students to develop some skills in observing crowds.

II.   **Theory**

The theoretical model used in this lecture is based on Clark McPhail's theoretical work. McPhail, writing in the symbolic interaction tradition, argues that the first step in the analysis of any crowd is the careful observation and description of the behavior of crowd members. He has developed a scheme for classifying most crowd behavior. A summary of his system is presented in the next section.

III.   McPhail's Crowd Classification System

Collective orientation

1. Clustering
2. Arcing, ringing
3. Gazing, facing
4. Vigiling

Collective vocalization

1. Ooh, ahh-, ohhing
2. Yeaing
3. Booing
4. Whistling
5. Hissing
6. Laughing
7. Wailing

Collective verbalization

1. Chanting
2. Singing
3, Praying
4. Reciting
5. Pledging

Collective gesticulation (nonverbal symbols)

1.   Roman salute (arm extended forward, palm down, fingers together)
2.   Solidarity salute (closed fist raised above the shoulder level)
3.   Digitus obscenus (fist raised, middle finger extended)
4.   #1 (fist raised shoulder level or above, index finger extended)
5.   Peace (fist raised, index finger and middle fingers separated and extended)
6.   Praise or victory (both arms fully extended overhead)

Collective vertical

1. Sitting
2. Standing
3. Jumping
4. Bowing
5. Kneeling
6. Kowtowing

Collective horizontal locomotion

1. Pedestrian clustering
2. Queuing
3. Surging
4. Marching
5. Jogging
6. Running

Collective manipulation

1. Applauding
2. Synchro-clapping
3. Finger snapping
4. Grasping, lifting, waving object
5. Grasping, lifting, throwing object
6. Grasping, lifting, pushing object

Adapted from C. McPhail, *The Myth of the Madding Crowd*, p. 164

IV. Analysis

First, go through each category and give a short illustration of the behavior. You can do this with both verbal and visual descriptions. Using slides or overheads of crowds taken from news magazines can be a good way to support the lecture. Next, ask your students to give examples of these behaviors that they have seen at sports crowds or rock concerts.

V. Application

The best application is to have your students actually observe crowds using the McPhail categories. A simple way to do this is to provide a handout based on section III and have your students identify the various types of behavior they see at the sporting event or rock concert. Another approach is to quantify the frequencies of behavior at a sporting event or rock concert.

VI. Resources

> McPhail, C., *The Myth of the Madding Crowd*. New York: Aldine De Gruyter, New York, (1991)
>
> Lewis, J. M. and A. Scarisbrick-Hauser, "An Analysis of Football Crowd Safety Reports Using The McPhail Categories" in R. Guilianotti, et al., *Football, Violence and Social Identity*, London: Routledge, (1994) forthcoming.

REFERENCES

Bricher, R. M., "Teaching Introductory Sociology: Using Aspects of The Classroom as Sociological Events". *Teaching Sociology*. 20:4 (October): 270-275.

Tolich, M., "Bringing Sociological Concepts Into Focus in the Classroom With *Modern Times*, *Roger and Me*, and *Annie Hall*." *Teaching Sociology*. 20:4 (October): 344-347.

SECTION FIVE
EXAMINATIONS

Examinations are very important. But they are generally not a happy part of our responsibilities as teachers. How to test students can cause a new teacher of the introductory sociology course a great deal of worry. Unfortunately, the ASA handbook does not deal with testing in any depth except to show formats on syllabi about test styles, grading and scheduling.

In this section of **TIPSTEACH**, I explicate a philosophy of examining introductory students by sharing with you four principles of examinations. For practical suggestions, ranging from when to examine to posting grades, I recommend you consult W. J. McKeachie, *Teaching Tips* (1978). Next, there is a discussion of publisher ancillaries for examinations. This is followed by a look at problems associated with designing examinations for introductory sociology students. The section concludes with some proposals for alternatives to traditional examinations.

Examination principles

It is possible to identify four principles for examining students. I call these the principles of fairness, completeness, triangulation, and promptness.

Fairness

Any examination must be fair. What does that mean? There are at least three criteria for fairness. First, there are course goals. Your examinations should reflect what you are trying to accomplish in your introductory sociology course. If it is your goal to get your introductory students using theory, your examinations should have questions that tap this knowledge.

Second, students need to have a temporal context for the examination. They should know exactly when examinations are going to be held and how long they will take. I am personally opposed to "pop" quizzes because of their punitive nature as well as the fact that they do not allow students preparation time.

Third, introductory students, as well as all students need to know, with explicit criteria, how the examination is going to be graded. For example, with multiple choice questions are there any weighting factors or do all questions count the same? Essay question criteria include, but are not limited to, such things as how complete an answer should be, how well it is to be written and what kinds of examples are expected. Whatever standards a professor develops, they need to be clearly communicated to students.

In summary, fairness is based on course goals, a knowledge of when examinations are going to be given and a clear articulation of grading standards.

Completeness

This principle refers to how comprehensive your examinations are going to be. Assume, for example, you are testing over four textbook chapters with sixty questions. Does this mean that fifteen questions come from each chapter? If this is not so, then students need to know the chapters you are emphasizing and those that are less important.

The second dimension of completeness has to do with text versus lectures. Most sociology teachers try to strike a balance between questions related to the lecture and those related to text. It is not always easy to do. I have no major formula, but have found that about sixty percent of the questions from the readings and forty percent from the lectures seems to work.

Triangulation

The idea of triangulation is that multiple testing methods provide better data on students than any single method. This is particularly true for examining introductory students. There are two types of triangulation. The "within method" encourages the teacher to use varieties of the same method in his or her test while the "between method" suggests distinctly different types of testing.

The Within Method

The within method suggests that when a professor examines with multiple choice tests, he or she should not rely just on four or five response questions. He or she should use several forms of multiple choice as well as matching and true-false questions, although it should be noted that most teachers do not like true-false questions. The teacher might have as one of his or her goals that students should have some knowledge of sociological classics. One form of the multiple choice question might be:

1.   Emile Durkheim is the author of

        A.   *Suicide.*
        B.   *The Protestant Ethic and the Spirit of Capitalism.*
        C.   *Capital.*
        D.   *Social Structure and Social Theory.*

The answer is A, *Suicide*. From a triangulation perspective, one might do an alternate question later in the test such as:

2.   The classic sociological study, *Suicide* was written by

        A.   Max Weber.
        B.   Emile Durkheim.
        C   Georg Simmel.
        D.   Karl Marx.

The answer, of course, is B, Emile Durkheim.

Another way to achieve within triangulation is to use matching questions. For example:

3.   Please match the sociological classic with its author.

Classic	Author
Suicide	A. Spencer
The Protestant Ethic and the Spirit of Capitalism	B. Durkheim
Capital	C. Marx
The Principles of Sociology	D. Weber

The order is A, B, C, and D (Just kidding to see if you were alert). It is B, D, C, and A.

True-false continues the within triangulation approach. For example:

> 4.   The author of *Suicide* is Max Weber.
>
>   A.   True
>   B.   False

The answer is B.

The Between Method

The between method proposes that professors use distinctly different approaches in examining introductory students. There are many ways to test other than with multiple choice questions including short answers, in class and take-home essays, and oral examinations. A between method of triangulation would combine any two of these methods for testing. Or, you would combine any one of these methods with multiple-choice testing. Let me say something about each method.

Short answer questions are less than an essay but more than a matching question. The length of a short answer question is typically from one to three sentences. For example, in regard to levels of measurement:

> 5.   What is a nominal scale? (See handout p. 29)
>
>   Possible Answer: A nominal scale is simple classification as illustrated by the church categories of Catholic, Protestant, and Jew. It is less precise (scientific) than an ordinal, interval or ratio scale.

The problem with short answer questions is that the answers can turn into longer essay questions and students can run out of time. You need to make your expectations as to the length of the answers clear in the test instructions.

In-class essay questions require longer treatments of subjects. The combination of essays is quite varied. Some professors like different levels of difficulty. On a fifty-point test, the first question might be worth ten points, the second fifteen points and the third twenty-five points. An example of this type of examination is presented in Figure I.

Figure I

Multi-valued Question Essay Test

<u>Introduction to Sociology</u>
EXAM II -- (Spring, 1994)

This test is worth twenty points. Answer three questions - two (2) questions from Set A and one (1) question from Set B. Be sure to use examples in your answers. Do not put your name on the bluebook, only your student ID. Please write your answers in a chronological order. I wish you well!

<u>SET A</u>: Answer any two questions. Each is worth five points.

1. What is naturalistic observation? How would you use it to study a sociology class help session being conducted in a campus restaurant?

2. What is the Thomas theorem? How would the definition of the situation influence a student's success or failure in a job?

3. What is civil inattention? Would this process occur in a shopping mall? Why? Be sure to use examples in your answer.

4. Noam Chomsky argues that there are linguistic universals as reflected in the ideas of surface structures versus deep structures of languages. Write an essay which reflects your understanding of these ideas.

<u>SET B</u>: Answer one question. It is worth 10 points.

1. Describe some incident you have seen on campus or at your work. Analyze the incident using the basic components of Goffman's dramaturgical model as presented in class.

2. Write three questions about going to see a professor in his or her office or going to an office in the student services center. The questions and the responses to them should be nominal, ordinal or interval for either attitude or behavior (intent) questions. You may use a combination of questions such as two attitude and one behavior (intent) question.

Other professors like to have essays of the same weight.

Figure II illustrates this type of test which I used for a mass class I teach. You should do whatever you think you will be the most comfortable grading.

Figure II
Single Valued Question Essay Test

INTRODUCTION TO SOCIOLOGY
(LEWIS)
STUDY GUIDE ESSAY TEST

STUDENT NAME: GRADE:
STUDENT ID.:   GRADER:

Please put your name (Last, first) and ID. on the scan sheet. Bubble in the circles. Answer ONE of the following questions. You will be graded on both content and writing. The test is worth 10% of your grade up to 25 points. You may use both sides of the answer sheet. Good luck! Answer one question.

A.   Ralph Linton writes, "The use of age as a reference point for establishing status is as universal as the use of sex[gender]." Write an essay using Linton's core concepts discussing this quote and applying it to life on the campus. Be sure to use examples in your essay.

OR

B.   Assume you are going to organize a campus sports booster club using Emile Durkheim's ideas. Would you train each member in all tasks (mechanical solidarity) or would you create a division of labor (organic solidarity)? Under what conditions would the promotion of mechanical solidarity versus organic solidarity be most effective?

Alternatives to the in-class essay examination are the open-book test and the take-home examination. These forms of testing are often used in upper division courses, but can be used with care in the introductory course. The open-book test is given in-class and students may use the textbooks or notes while taking the test. Often beginning students will use the "open" aspects incorrectly by spending too much of the examination period "studying" rather than drawing on material already learned. Or they will simply copy considerable amounts of the textbook and/or notes into the test. This may evaluate motor ability, but not learning or, more importantly, thinking.

Take-home essays are simply an extension of the in-class essay format. Likely, you will not use this type of essay format unless you are teaching an introductory course with a small number of students such as one offered by an Honors college in a University or at a small liberal college such as Hiram or Oberlin in Ohio. A take-home essay reduces the pressure of the examination environment which is probably its biggest advantage. There are, however, several disadvantages. First, the examinations are much longer making the grading more difficult. Second, you cannot control for student "consulting" on the examination. Third, students who procrastinate lose the advantage of reducing the pressure of the testing environment when they write the examination under hurried conditions. Fourth, you may get telephone calls or office visits seeking assistance. These requests are legitimate. You need to figure out a way that all students can easily contact you. When I give a take-home examination, I schedule office hours for questions well before the due date of the examination.

Promptness

The principle of promptness refers to a simple but important factor for examinations. That is, students want to know as soon as possible how they did on the examination. Often they will ask what is your "turn around time" on tests. Very few sociologists have not had the experience of giving a test in the morning and being asked in the afternoon if it was graded yet. Try to plan your schedule so that you can get tests with scores back to students within a week. Multiple-choice tests are usually quickly graded by machine scoring or a manually used key and promptness should be easy to achieve.

The principle of promptness is likely more often violated with essay examinations and, of courses, term papers. One way to ease the prompt return of essay examinations is to think through the answers ahead of time. Under the pressures of busy schedules we are tempted to knock out a quick set of essay questions without thinking through standards for evaluation and grading. If you think through the answers ahead of time you are likely to get tests back in a prompt and orderly manner.

Joseph Janes and Diane Hauer (1988) have developed some practical suggestions for grading essay tests and, by extension, term papers that, if followed, will simplify the prompt return of these materials to introductory students. Drawing on their (Hauer and Janes, 1988: p. 127) nine principles, I propose the four "C's of grading: compassionately, carefully, clearly and constructively.

1.   Compassionately. Don't be sarcastic or arrogant. Try to conclude your marking with a generally positive overview assessment of the student's work.

2.   Carefully. Be sure to score each essay question or dimension of the paper carefully and add the scores accurately.

3.   Clearly. Mark clearly so that the student knows which points were desirable which ones were clearly wrong.

4.   Constructively. Try to conclude your grading with suggestions for improvement by pointing out future lines of inquiry that might be developed on the basis of your student's answer on the essay. Keys to the student interests lie in her or his examples on the test.

Linked to the principle of promptness is the handing back of examinations. There are many ideas on this. I give back my examinations at the end of the class period. If you hand them back at the start of the hour, students with good grades will selectively perceive your lecture because they are so pleased. Students with poor grades will not listen because they are angry and/or upset. This may sound simplistic, but I think there is some truth to the selective perception idea. I try to be available for appointments on the day I return tests.

Publisher Ancillaries for Examinations

If you adopt a textbook as part of your introductory course, then you should consult with the publisher's representative for ancillaries that can be used in examinations. Most publishers provide a test bank on disk as well as in hard copy. There are many types of questions in a test bank including multiple choice (multiple-guess in undergraduate jargon) true-false, matching, short answer and essay. The questions are written to get at ideas, facts and applications often with degrees of difficulty such as easy, moderate and difficult. I have heard that some publishers are thinking of giving validity and reliability data on questions but I have not yet seen this happen.

Here are some examples of questions that test conceptual, factual and application knowledge on the subject of social groups a topic dear to the hearts of most of us. Many examples are modifications of questions from an excellent text bank prepared by Reba Rowe Lewis (no relation) for Jon M. Shepard's 1993 *Sociology* (fifth edition) from West Publishing. **Conceptual** knowledge questions are usually definitions. For example:

1.   Sociologists define a _____ that is impersonal and task-oriented and involves only a segment of the lives and personalities of its members.

A. secondary group
B. primary group
C. control group
D. peer group

The answer is A, secondary group.

This is a very good question for several reasons. It requires the student to know something in detail. First, the wrong answers, called distractors, are attractive. That is, they are clearly plausible. For example, the student has to know the difference between a primary group and secondary group.

Second, the student has to understand why a peer group does not meet the definition that is provided. Third, the student has to remember that a "control group" is not a secondary group, but is a term used in the description of experimental designs.

A **fact** question gets at a student's knowledge about concrete information. For example,

2.   According to the table in the text what percentage of total profits do the top one hundred American corporations earn?

A.   20%
B.   30%
C.   70%
D.   54%

The answer is C, 70%.

This questions measures factual knowledge as well as the skill of extracting data from tables.

An **application** question asks students to take a concept and interpret a social situation using it. Typically, students have more trouble with application questions than with concept or fact questions. Here is an example of an application question.

3.   Which of the following examples is <u>least</u> likely to be a secondary group?

A   manager and his professional baseball team.

B   professor and students.

C   a marine recruit and his drill instructor.

D.   a married couple

The answer is D, a married couple.

This question is an application question because it requires the student to decide the best answer for several types of social situations. In other words, the student has to think about all four responses before he or she answers "D."

Writing Multiple Choice Questions

Having written many multiple choice tests I can attest (nice pun) to the difficulties of writing valid and reliable multiple choice questions.

If you use a publisher test bank, most of your own question writing will be based on your lectures or modifying the test bank. Here are a few practical suggestions for writing multiple choice questions.

One, carefully write the stem (the first part of the question preceding answers) as clearly as possible. Answers come easy. The success of a good multiple choice question lies in the stem.

Two, make the distractors (wrong answers) as plausible as possible. My own failing is to go for humorous distractors such as "The Heisenberg principle is the top school official in a small German high school." No doubt students enjoy these interludes but the result is the question becomes easier.

Three, give equal weight to answer positions A to D or F. Some professors try to randomize this, but I think care in using all four or five positions solves the problem.

Lastly, avoid trick questions. They probably don't measure as well as straight forward questions; they take more time to write; and they made students angry.

Cheating on Examinations

It seems appropriate to conclude this section of **TIPSTEACH** with some thoughts about the most difficult thing professors face in examining students - cheating. I think this is primarily a problem with the mass class, but it can happen in smaller classes. Interestingly those writing about the teaching of the introductory sociology course have little to say about the topic. Goldsmid and Wilson, for example, (1980: pp. 327-328) have less than a page on the topic and Campbell, et al. (1985) have nothing to say on the issue. I could not find any article in *Teaching Sociology* that addressed this topic for the introductory course. Psychologists seem to write more about the issues than sociologists.

Let me review what may be the major issues involved in examination cheating. They are preexamination security, cheating during the test and using old test forms.

Because of the difficulty involved in writing multiple-choice questions, work on them has to be done well ahead of the examination date. If the production of the test involves staff, then the deadlines are even longer. Tests laying around are tempting targets for misguided students. Simple care should prevent this from happening by keeping drafts and final copies in file cabinets. Teachers should also be sensitive on this issue regarding computer security as well. The department chairpersons and/or secretary can give you some guidance on this.

Most cheating goes on during the test. I think the only solution is aggressive proctoring. This usually solves the problem or potential problem in smaller classes.

Using old tests can be a tricky problem. Some professors try to aggressively control all copies of a test with complex coding systems or other forms of policing. They do this so that they can use the same test repeatedly semester after semester. It is hard to achieve complete control particularly as the class gets bigger. Thus, it is difficult to assume that old tests have not gotten into the hands of current students.

Professors may want to hand a test back for pedagogical reasons. That is, students can learn from reviewing tests to see what items they did well on or what items they missed.

Third, there are many ways tests can get to students. For example, some professors using the ancillary capabilities of publishers put the entire test bank on files that are accessible to students. It is possible, though difficult, to copy questions that could be used in future classes.

There are also simple mistakes. I once walked down the hall in my building and found the hard copy of a test bank in a waste basket of a doctoral student who was leaving for the summer and was cleaning out his office.

I think that unless you go to great efforts to control tests, you are going to have to assume that some copies have gotten out to future students in your class. This is not so serious a problem if you are using a textbook because the ancillary test programs have many more questions than you could possible use up. The programs for designing tests are generally user friendly. Of course, you still have the burden of writing new lecture questions. This is easily facilitated by putting in new lectures each semester, which might not be a bad idea. A new lecture adds vitality to your course.

This section of **TIPSTEACH** has presented some principles of testing for the introductory sociology course. A strategy for grading the essay test was suggested with four principles. The section concluded with a discussion on designing multiple choice questions and problems associated with cheating on examinations.

The next two sections of **TIPSTEACH** look at alternatives to examinations.   The next section examines class projects and the following one discusses the place of the field project in introductory sociology.

REFERENCES

Campbell, F. L., Blalock, H. M. Jr., and McGee, R. 1985. *Teaching Sociology: The Quest for Excellence*. Chicago: Nelson-Hall.

Goldsmid C. and Wilson, E. K., 1980. *Passing on Sociology: The Teaching of a Discipline*. Belmont, CA: Wadsworth.

Janes, J. and Hauer, D. 1988. *Now What: Readings on Surviving (and Even Enjoying) Your First Experience at College Teaching*. Second Edition. Littleton, Mass.: Copley Publishing Group.

Lewis, R. R. 1993. Test Bank to Accompany *Sociology*, Fifth Edition, by Jon Shepard. Minneapolis/St. Paul: West.

McKeachie, W. J. 1978. *Teaching Tips: A Guidebook for the Beginning College Teacher.* Seventh Edition. Lexington, Mass.: D. C. Heath.

Shepard, J. 1993. *Sociology*. Fifth Edition. Minneapolis/St. Paul: West.

SECTION SIX
CLASS EXERCISES

Introduction

This section of **TIPSTEACH** provides you with thirty workable projects for active class learning. They are designed to illustrate a sociological principle or two and to have some fun in class. They should generate discussion and debate. I have used some form of the projects in my classes. Some of them appear in alternative forms in one or both of two instructor's manuals I have written.[1] I conclude each exercise by linking it to one or more of the four principles that follow.

Class Exercises

As Everett Wilson notes in his syllabus check list, teachers of the introductory course need to think about the active learning dimensions of their classes. Over the years I have developed many class exercise projects which encourage active learning. It seems to me that there are four questions you need to ask about any class exercise you plan to use.

First, how does the class exercise fit into your course goals? What are you trying to accomplish with this exercise? Are you simply illustrating a sociological idea, or are you trying to accomplish a more difficult task of creating a social situation that can be critically analyzed?

Second, can the exercise be conducted easily and efficiently? The instructor should note whether the exercise requires much preparation with handouts, overheads, classroom modifications and so forth. If it does, then you need to ask yourself if the exercise is worth it.

Third, how are you going to evaluate the students' learning in terms of this exercise? For example, are you going to take a mechanical approach of evaluating simple participation in the exercise without getting into qualitative evaluations? That is, 100% participation leads to an "A", 80% to a "B" and so forth. Or are you going to judge the class exercise subjectively on how well the students contribute? Sometimes it is possible to have students grade each other's participation. This has to be done with considerable care in order not to create disharmony among class members.

Fourth, is the exercise fun? This is not to say everything you do in a class has to be entertaining. Sometimes it is necessary to put your nose to the grindstone and work hard. But in class exercises I think there should always be an element of fun. I believe this fun will not interfere with the point you are trying to make.

The exercises that follow are presented as they would logically come in a conventional introductory course. For convenience I have tied the exercises to specific subject areas, but they likely could be used in with a variety of topics. They can be done by the beginning teacher with ease.

THE FIRST DAY

On the first day of class it is particularly important that one gets a good start. It seems to me that there are three C's that are important to the first day. The three C's are community, concern and comedy. First, you want to tell your students that they are in a community of scholars. That is, they will be working together on the various aspects of sociology. Second, you are concerned about their success as sociology students. You want them to do well. Sociologists are notorious institution bashers. At times this is appropriate, but not in the introductory class on the first day. Lastly, the third "C," comedy, reminds students that studying sociology is fun.

Exercise 1

Have students fill out cards providing some background on their hometown, father and mother's occupation or job, their phone number and any other information that you deem important. After the cards are completed have the student get a telephone number or two from those who are sitting nearby. This will save you time because students can call the student for missed assignments and notes.

Ask the student to interview the person from whom they got the telephone number, for some sociological information. You can either give out the questions, i.e., religion, size of family, or parents' occupations, or let the students come up with questions.

This is a very efficient project and easily done. It can be completed in a short time and all you need to bring is three by five cards. It begins the process of creating community because there is at least one other student who knows who they are in the class. By the way, look for recycled cards. Kent State's library just put its card catalogue on-line and I am using the recycled cards for this project.

THEORY

With a theory exercise you are trying to get the student to understand the applicability of theoretical analysis. Your students need to understand that the theories appearing in a text are useful and not just abstract academic exercises. I like to point out that the three perspectives of structural-functionalism, conflict and interactionism will appear throughout the text.

Exercise 2

Ask students to read all or part of a novel such as A. Huxley's **Brave New World** or George Orwell's *1984* and have them interpret the types of societies using F. Toennies' *Gemeinschaft/Gesellschaft* or E. Durkheim's mechanical or organic solidarity found in the novels. You can all discuss the novels from a conflict or interactionist perspective. Both novels are useful for illustrating sociological processes of socialization, deviance or stratification. Short stories also work in this assignment. For example, O. Henry's, "The Gift of the Magi" is a wonderful and sad illustration of the role-taking problems.

This exercise fits into the course goal of tying the introductory sociology course into a general liberal arts education. If students do not like the two novels that are proposed, ask them to come with suggestions for novels or short stories of their own.

Exercise 3

Have students bring in personal advertisements from the local newspapers. In small groups, have the students analyze the advertisement using interactionist theory. Do women present different symbolic traits than men in the advertisements? If yes, why is this the case? You might tie this exercise into some of Erving Goffman's work.

Many instructor's manuals tie projects into newspaper assignments. This project encourages the introductory students to apply critical thinking using sociological ideas to the evaluation of press reports.

Exercise 4

Students are not always comfortable with the idea that social interaction can be understood as theater. Begin by reviewing the basic ideas of dramaturgical theory including impression management teams and audiences, adornments, props and front and back regions. A useful way to teach Goffman's dramaturgical model is to compare analyze a family event such as wrapping Christmas presents or other holiday activities. Is there a place where the wrapping goes on that is a back region? Is there a place for giving presents that can be interpreted as a front region?

This project is easy to do and can get students thinking about the practical aspects of social life associated with important family rituals.

Exercise 5

Current events can be used to show the applicability of theory. The August 30, 1993 issue of *Newsweek* reported the case of Kimberly Mays the teenager who successfully divorced her biological parents (Ernest and Regina Twigg). She did this by receiving a ruling from the judge that she could not be forced to visit her biological parents (she had been mistakenly separated from them at birth). This case is likely to be in the public arena for several years as the biological parents have said that they will appeal the ruling. Invite your students to write a short essay interpreting the ruling using one or more of the structural-functional, conflict, or interactionist perspectives. You might want to use a more current event than this one for the assignment.

In thinking about writing assignments, you need to think through how you are going to evaluate the written work. What weights are you going to give to theory, analysis and writing should be determined before this or any other assignment if given? You might want to check the section on grading projects elsewhere in **TIPSTEACH**.

RESEARCH METHODS

With these lectures the introductory teacher is developing an appreciation for empirical methods and results.

Exercise 6

Teach students how to use census data. Conduct a discussion on why this data can be interpreted as social facts after Emile Durkheim's ideas. I have had good discussions about the rates of drowning which sadly have been remarkably consistent over the years. I focus on risk taking behavior and social structural elements that encourage it, i.e. being a young male.

This exercise has to be done with care, because of the possible pain it might cause some students who might have had some recent experiences with friends or relatives who have been killed or seriously injured by accidents.

Exercise 7

Polls are always being printed in the newspapers. Ask students to bring one in to evaluate for question design and bias. Encourage them to write questions as alternatives to the ones in the poll. You can also get into the issues related to levels of measurement if you want to do so. (See Hoover handout, p. 28).

The value of this exercise lies in its facilitation of critical thinking by introductory students which is seen as an important goal in recent thinking and writing on teaching sociology.

Exercise 8

Most introductory textbooks have sections on validity and reliability. These are very difficult ideas for beginning students to understand. You might want to design a project on the idea of validity and reliability using some campus topic. For example, the impact of "hate" incidents on campuses which seem to be appearing more frequently on college and university campuses. Ask students to decide what a valid measure of "impact" and "hate" would be. Conclude by linking the validity analysis to issues of reliability on the hate incident.

This exercise ties the sociological imagination into critical thinking about campus problems. It also shows that sociologists are arm-chair philosophers. That is, we try to bring empirical evidence of some type to bear on our theoretical analyses.

Exercise 9

I think that students who take Introductory Sociology should develop their observational skills. Help them design a direct observation study of some popular gathering place on campus. Set up teams of students to do the observing as public gathering places on campus such as student centers, sporting arenas or commons. You can use class time to develop the observational categories of observing and practicing the recording of data. Have the teams report their findings back to your class.

This assignment is fun. In addition, it encourages your student to see life on campus in a different light.

Exercise 10

Ethnographic interviews can be of great interest to students particularly if they are involved with people who have been active in social movements or in events related to social movements.

A colleague who teaches a course in Vietnam history has his students do ethnographic interviews with veterans of the war. These interviews provide students with considerable insight into the war. Another type of ethnographic interview looks at people involved in social problems either as a victim or as a helper or both. For example, you might encourage your students to look at drug using from the perspective of a user or someone who is trying to help. This assignment can develop into a term paper or generate significant class discussion.

This is not an easy assignment to do because some universities may require human subject review procedures with this type of interview. You should check with appropriate authorities before giving students this assignment.

CULTURE

All introductory texts make the distinction between social structure and culture. It is important to get students thinking about this distinction. One way to do this is to do an exercise on subcultures.

Exercise 11

Graffiti on campus may suggest the presence of a subculture on campus or in the local community. Have students classify the graffiti types by location and content. For example, **location** might be public versus non public, walls versus desks, classroom building versus non classroom. The **content** of graffiti might be oriented toward the political, erotic, popular culture, sport, humor or local campus concerns. Discuss with your students whether the data point to a subculture on campus. This exercise can also be used when you deal with deviance.

Exercise 12

Show your students a film such as *Moonstruck* (Italian-American families) or *Witness* (Amish families). These films and related ones are easy to rent and showing them without charge does not violate the fair usage provisions of the copyright laws. Discuss with them what seems accurate about the film and what may be stereotypical in terms of sub cultures. For a feature length film I would give my students a handout in advance. This would have a film synopsis along with discussion questions to encourage work following the showing of the film.

SOCIAL STRUCTURE

One common denominator of an introductory course is the linkage between the analysis of culture and social structure. Texts, lecture and projects all do this by linking the ideas of status and role and primary and secondary groups. The following exercises are designed to explicate the culture and social structure linkage.

Exercise 13

The idea that a person lives in status and role sets is a useful way to get your students to be introspective about the forces that shape their lives. Review with your students your own status-role sets. Try to give as much detail as you feel comfortable with doing. Students don't mind the fact that their sociology professor is a human being. You can build on some sharing that you might have done in the opening lecture.

Exercise 14

Related to the notions of status and role are the ideas of role strain and conflict. These are not always clear to students. Explore the ideas of strain and conflict using this story that came out of 1960's political movements as an illustration of sexist attitudes. The story: In California a man and his son left for a hiking and camping trip in the mountains. After about an hour they were in a terrible truck and car accident. The father went to one hospital. The son went to another one. As he was being rolled into surgery, the doctor said, "I cannot operate. This is my son." Why? Of course, the surgeon was the patient's mother. Not recognizing this may suggest that one might be stereotyping in thinking about "appropriate" occupations for women. Incidently you might tell your students that both father and son survived the crash.

Here there is no role conflict or strain because the social system of medicine has developed clear norms about how a surgeon should treat one of her children. Discuss with your students why these rules have to be clear to both patient and doctor?

Additional discussion questions:

a.   What would the physician have done if the patient had been her husband?
b.   What would the physician have done in either case if there were no other physicians available?
c.   Are these norms generalizable to other professions such as law and teaching?

This assignment generates considerable discussion so you should be prepared to use most of the period for it.

GROUPS

In the analysis of groups, students should become aware of how group structures shape their lives. One way to do this is to develop exercises about groups that draw on classroom dynamics. For example, breaking into small buzz (discussion) groups allow one to talk about structure of the group and how it works in classroom discussions and exercises.

Exercise 15

Have students bring in newspaper stories that can be interpreted using reference group behavior. For example, wedding announcements from the *New York Times* could be used in this assignment. Try to get your students to think about whether they use membership or non membership reference groups for normative or comparative standards (Merton, 1968 *passim*).

SOCIALIZATION

Most discussions of socialization entail some thinking about teaching and learning in groups. Sociologists often describe aspects of teaching and learning in terms of direct teaching, role modeling and imitation.

Exercise 16

It is useful to get students thinking about how people learn. One way to do this is to have your students become teachers and learners in class. Have students in your course teach other students a skill such as sewing, some sport skill, or a game (card games and tricks are particularly fun). Next, have the students discuss whether the socialization process involved behavior, attitudes, or emotions, or a combination of all three.

Exercise 17

Any lectures on socialization should encourage students to be introspective. I use the handout on p. 9 to illustrate this. I have students fill out the handout before class in consultation with their parents or older siblings. In class the students share their investigations with fellow students. They are amazed to see similarities particularly among media favorites. After this is completed, students are encouraged to write an essay, for extra credit, using ideas from the textbook and lectures for an analysis of their socialization experiences.

Exercise 18

Ask students to list all the socialization experiences they have had within the last week. Have them discuss what would happen if they had not learned what they were supposed to do in a class, a job or social event. This assignment also lends itself to a diary assignment where you have students track and analyze socialization experiences. A good diary assignment should cover about three weeks of time. One difficulty of diary assignments is that they require a considerable amount of time to grade.

DEVIANCE

In most traditional sociology courses we tend to move from discussions of culture and socialization to deviance issues. I believe beginning students should understand both the structural and processes aspects of deviance.

Exercise 19

During half of your lectures, have students take notes with something other than a pen or pencil. Crayons work, as do magic markers. It shows to your students their commitments to technology. Also, they become deviants. Sometimes students even "cheat" and use normal note-taking procedures. Using pen and paper as alternatives to hand calculators to do simple math problems is a useful project as well.

Exercise 20

Using breaching experiments, have your students violate some spatial norm in the student cafeteria or library. Having two students, working as a team, sitting too close to a stranger works well. After a few minutes, tell the students to stop the experiment and explain the breaching experiment to the subject. Have your students interpret the responses using Goffman's dramaturgical theory in either written or oral report. You should have an alternative assignment for students who find this one difficult to do. A good test of this is to do a form of the assignment yourself. If you feel comfortable with it, it is likely that your students will also. You should be aware of the fact that some sociologists, in recent years, have raised questions about the ethics of breaching experiments.

SOCIAL STRATIFICATION

Typically we want to accomplish three things with introductory lectures in stratification. First, we want to show how societies stratify using Weber's analysis of class, status and party. Second, we want to show the students the issues around the measurement of stratification variables. Lastly, we want to give them a sense of the debate associated with the structural-functional and conflict perspectives on social stratifications.

Exercise 21

Have students design a questionnaire which gets at the ways to measure social class dimensions. You might want to break your class into three subgroups with each group using one method. You might tie the class into methodology as well as issues related to levels of measurement. A word of warning is needed. This assignment can use considerable class time as the students get into the assignment.

Exercise 22

Have students develop panels where they take the parts of other status communities discussing political issues. For example, the "male" panel (all women) and the "female" (all men) talking about sexual harassment. Or, students might develop a panel as elderly people discussing voting on a school levy. Students should be encouraged to be sensitive to other students in their role-playing. An alternative would be to have students write an in-class exercise on how their ascribed status is shaped by society. However, have women write as men and men as women. You might begin with a general discussion of the assignment before the writing starts. As an alternative you might have students write as an 80 year old man or woman. Conclude the assignment with a general discussion of problems the students had with writing as an alternative ascribed status. A word of warning: This project can be painful to some students. Be willing and prepared to have a conference with students who want to explore their feelings about the stereotypes that other students might report in the course of the discussions.

SOCIAL INSTITUTIONS

Conventional introductory courses tend to look at the five universal institutions of family, education, economy, religion, the polity. Recently, textbooks have added two more institutions to this list - the health system and mass communication. All textbooks cover these areas. Sociologists are trying to do two basic things when we analyze these institutions for our students. First, we are trying to get them to see how these institutions shape their lives. Second, we are moving them to a position of objectivity so that they can analytically look at the impact of institutions on their lives and the lives of others. In a sense, studying institutional impact is one of the most powerful expressions of the sociological imagination.

FAMILY

Exercise 23

Have students organize a panel of speakers to talk about the joys and sorrows of being nonmarried persons in American society. The speakers could represent a variety of perspectives including a single parent, a widow or widower, or a person who voluntarily chose not to marry. As an alternate or companion to this project have students bring in married couples in various stages of the family life cycle as reflected in the text. Have students prepare questions before the class to ask the couples. Four or five couples is about the right number to have for a panel. Be sure to send thank you notes to the couples who participate.

Exercise 24

Health insurance problems heavily influence the family. The April 28, 1991 issue of the *New York Times* reported that 33 million Americans lack health insurance protection. This is thirteen percent of the population. You might invite a speaker from the AMA and/or local medical and dental associations to talk about the professionalization and specialization of medicine. You might want to tie this presentation into a discussion or debate by students on the national health insurance programs. As an alternative you might assign a term paper to your students to look at the national health insurance programs from either functionalist or conflict perspectives. The national news magazines regularly carry articles on the proposed programs as does the *New York Times*.

EDUCATION

Exercise 25

Open your lecture by reviewing the ideas of the latent and manifest functions. Next, explore some latent functions of the college and university life in relation to the marriage market. Have your students come up with a college or university experience that encourages meeting people who could be possible mates. For example, studying together, working on term projects or panels as parts of course requirements would be examples. Follow this up with an analysis of non academic experiences that bring potential marriage partners together. This includes such things as sorority and fraternity pledging or working at a college or university. Students should be surprised by the number of opportunities to meet potential marriage partners. Students are fascinated with the ideas of the hidden curriculum. Ask students to investigate the informal norms of the classroom as they vary from discipline to discipline. Are there different sets of norms because of class size or the level of class (lower versus upper division)? Point out that there are mechanisms for learning the norms and sanctions for not following them.

RELIGION

Exercise 26

Show the film *Inherit the Wind* (1960) which was based on Jerome Laurence's play of the same name to your class. It was based on the John Scopes trial and there are wonderful performances by Frederic March and Spencer Tracy. It should stimulate interesting discussions about evolution, creationism and the interests of the media and the public. This also ties in nicely with discussion of the political institution. You might want to interpret the film using ideas of Weber and Durkheim on religion. If you don't want to use the entire film, show the section where "Darrow" puts "Bryant" on the stand.

POLITY

Exercise 27

Political cartoons in newspapers generally assume some knowledge by readers. Have students bring in political cartoons from either a campus paper or a local one and discuss with them the symbols and jokes that would be understood by local readers only.

Contrast this analysis with cartoons from a national paper or news magazine.

MASS MEDIA

The mass media, particularly television, are the voices of the institutions of society. Many sociologists use the ideas of agenda setting to talk about the media. Agenda setting argues that the media tell us when and what to think about the civil discourse of society.

Exercise 28

Ask students to review their own experiences with the Persian Gulf War by writing a retrospective diary on their television viewing experiences with it. You might want to provide some empirical cues from national news magazines. Have your students include in the diary whether they were CNN junkies of the war as were many Americans. If they had relatives or friends involved in the war, in whatever way, this should be part of the diary. This assignment should get students thinking about their own vicarious participation in the Gulf War.

COLLECTIVE BEHAVIOR AND SOCIAL MOVEMENTS

Exercise 29

Gossip and rumor appear as part of collective discussion in textbooks. A good way to show how gossip and rumor works is to analyze how students build accounts using unverified information. Building on Exercise 28, you might have students write about rumor and gossip associated with the Persian Gulf War.

Another way to study rumor and gossip is to examine its place on a college or university campus. Students often use rumors and gossip to explain actions of others in the campus community. For example, a professor may refuse to allow a student the chance to make up a quiz when the student failed to notify the professor before the quiz is given. An account based on rumor or gossip may be developed that the professor does not like the student because he is a member of a sorority or fraternity or is an athlete.

Alternatively, the student might develop an account, based on rumor or gossip, that the professor didn't get a raise (a very realistic possibility) and therefore doesn't want to do any additional work. Point out to your students that attributions and accounts can be and often are based on gossip and rumor. Therefore, students are acting on the basis of information that is likely to be absolutely false or certainly unverified.

THE LAST DAY OF CLASS

Exercise 30

The last day of class is very important. Try to provide a summary of the class and what you expected of them. Discuss with your students the final and what it will cover. Indicate whether you will be in your office after the final is given and the days and times (Be sure to honor these days and times). Tell your students how you can be reached in the following semester in case they have questions about their grade or the course.

Notes

1. The instructor's manuals were written for:
   Boudreau, F. A. and newman, W. M., *Understanding Social Life*, West 1993.
   Thompson, W. E. and Hickey, J. V., *Society in Focus*, HarperCollins, 1993.

SECTION SEVEN
THE RESEARCH PROJECT

Introduction

The previous section has presented thirty active learning exercises for the introductory class. Section Seven proposes an active learning project that is more complex than the exercises presented in the previous section. This is the introductory course research project. Most sociologists like to have some form of active learning experience in their upper division courses. Often this takes the form of a research project. But it is also possible to do it in the introductory course. Can "intro" students do research? I once asked A. Paul Hare, a well known small group expert, if he missed having graduate students when he taught at Haverford College in Pennsylvania. He said, "Jerry, you have bright people around you that you call graduate students, I have bright people that I call sophomores." With some guidance (and a little courage) I believe you can get introductory students doing research projects that result in creative pieces of sociological scholarship.

I have my students study sociological episodes which I define as micro social events having clear beginnings and endings. For example, a social episode might range from the exchange that takes place between a fast food customer and the clerk or child care behavior at a mall.

There are three assumptions about studying the social episode. First, many events in social life have clear beginnings and endings. Second, the sociology student can benefit by learning about these events. That is, understanding the episode and the societal response to it brings the student a fuller insight into social structure. Third, studying the episode allows undergraduates to develop research skills including the developing of theoretical formulations, observational skills, collecting data, interpreting of data and writing up findings.

I start developing research attitudes early in the semester. In the second week of semester I ask students to give me a sample of their best writing. This achieves two things. First, it tells the student that I am serious about writing. Second, it gives them a sense of my expectations for writing. This request to see their previous work is what I call a **reporting point**. There are others during the course including a short proposal on their topic stating what they want to study and why they want to study it, an outline of the paper, a progress report on the paper, a short lecture on writers' block and turning in the paper. Let's look at these in more detail.

Researching the Episode

To research the episode you should take your students through nine different stages as they research the episode:

Reporting point 1. In the second week of the semester (you would have to make some adaptations for the quarter system), I ask for a sample of writing from previous classes. For fall semester, first year students, this may be a challenge so I accept a short essay based on the first chapter of the textbook. I am looking for writing problems such as spelling, paragraph logic, and syntax.

Reporting point 2. This occurs early in the course. After two weeks (on a semester system), I have finished lectures on theory and methods. I ask the students to give a verbal statement on what type of episode they would like to study. Responses are in three categories. First, there are very general responses such as behavior at malls or in fast food stores. Second, there are general responses in terms of processes such as the effect of rude (or polite behavior) of bus drivers. Third, specific topics such as "Why do Sears clerks say 'Have a nice day' at the end of a sale?" At this point students are not committed to any project. However, the exercise does stimulate thinking about a topic.

Reporting point 3. This takes place just before the first examination as part of a test help session. Students are divided into "genre groups" of related topics. Thus, students who are going to study mall behavior are in one group while the "bar" students are in another and the family gatherings, such as Thanksgiving, are in a third group. A fourth or fifth genre group might be related to specific events on your campus.

At Kent State, in the Fall, we have Halloween Night in downtown Kent where students dress in costumes. This happens on many campuses (Shelly, Anderson and Mattley, 1992). It is a wonderful venue for introductory research projects.

Reporting point 4. At this stage students have heard lectures of theory and methods and have read the appropriate chapters on these topics in the text. They are placed into genre groups, now called buzz groups, and asked to present their project and theoretical approach to the other "intro" students in the group. After the buzz groups are finished, each student briefly presents her or his project and its theoretical approach to the class in very general terms. The effect of this exercise is to force the students to think in theoretical terms about a sociological research question.

As far as a theoretical approach, students can draw on any number of theoretical perspectives. Erving Goffman's ideas are popular as well as elements of exchange theory. Durkheim's ideas on ritual are useful for the study of family gatherings.

Reporting point 5. After a brief lecture on the structure of a research proposal, I organize the class into a workshop to write a rough draft of their proposals. The format of the proposal is as follows:

1. Statement of the research question
2. Theoretical approach
   a. Hypotheses
3. Research methods (triangulation)
4. Expected results
5. Bibliography

This proposal format is a traditional one for sociologists. Two comments are in order. First, students have difficulties moving from a general theoretical framework to formal hypotheses. You need to devote class time showing students how to formulate hypotheses.

Second, the idea of triangulation is relatively new to students. I conclude lectures on methods with remarks on triangulation. These remarks are based on an article I wrote on the subject (Lewis, 1986). It argues that competent sociological research requires a multiple method approach including site visits, personal interviews, newspaper articles, photographs and films, and official documents. This lecture has been presented earlier under the methodology section. Students are expected to support their participant observations with at least one other data source such as a brief content analysis of a newspaper or an in-depth interviews with a few respondents.

The workshop activities are straightforward. I ask the students to begin with the research question. Students work in teams of two or three. I propose questions and they answer them in writing after discussing the questions with other students. Thus, students would be asked: "What is your research question?" The student might write, "Why do fast food people close the transaction with 'Have a nice day?'" Or "What are the functions of Thanksgiving day dinner?" Next, I ask: "What is your theoretical approach?" Typically, the student, by now, will have an idea of what he or she wants to do. So the student writes a paragraph or two on his or her theoretical concerns.

After a few minutes of work, I ask volunteers to read their research questions to the class. We briefly discuss each question that has been presented, but with the ground rule that you can only say something positive about it. I have to be careful because it is easy to fall into a negative critical stance which is so much part of the review process in sociology. The class proceeds on through the rest of the proposal. This work can be completed in a fifty minute period.

About a week after the workshop, students hand in a proposal for the research project. Typically it runs two to three pages although it can be longer. I read the proposals making suggestions on how they can be improved. My comments typically focus on types of data that they have or have not included in the proposal. I return the proposals as soon as possible because the students are quite anxious about my responses to it. The mistake students made most often at this stage is the omission for obvious data sources that support the participant observation. For example, a student might not realize that he can use city government data such as health board information as sources of material on patterns of illness in a city.

Reporting Point 6. Students are excused from class for a week to work on their projects. During this week I ask them to set up a conference with me to discuss their research. Typically the conference lasts from ten to twenty minutes. While it can range over a variety of topics, three issues are typical.

First, students are concerned with how to relate the triangulation to their research. That is, have they truly met the standard of two data sources? I try to point out to them that the triangulation model is an ideal to be strived for in one's research. Second, they need suggestions on how to relate the data that they have gathered to the theoretical model that they are using. If it is Goffman, I try to show how one can relate empirical evidence to his concepts such as the back or front region. Third, they want to know how to write up their projects and I tell them that I will be explaining this in more detail in class using a sample article. If they don't want to wait, I tell them to go to the library and read some sociology journals for examples of how to write up the research. *Social Problems* is an excellent resource for protocol articles. Typically, the student has only one conference, but I have had students who have talked with me at almost every stage of the project.

FIGURE I
HANDOUT FOR TERM PAPER

INTRODUCTION TO SOCIOLOGY
(LEWIS)
SPRING 1994
TERM PAPER OUTLINE

I. Title page

II. Introduction

This section tells what the researcher does in the paper. It is an introduction to the entire paper.

III. Theory

This section is an introduction to the theory or theories used in the paper. In a sense it is an "introduction" to theory. When you discuss the theory (or theories) be sure to use examples, but not from the empirical problem you are researching. That is, don't do your analysis in this section.

IV. Data Sources

This section of the paper describes the various ways the researcher collected data. **No** detail is unimportant. You may wish to include an appendix to support this section. For example, the bill from a fast food place.

V. Narrative

In this section you describe what you observed. Be sure to reflect the temporal dimension of the event in some way. When did things happen in the event you are researching? (See Heysel paper)

VI. Analysis

In this section, the researcher brings together theory, narrative and data interpreting the social episode along lines we have been discussing in class.

VII. Endnotes

As appropriate, but be sure to give a citation for all direct quotes including interviews.

VIII. Annotated bibliography

Reporting point 7. Here, I do most of the work by helping students with their writing. This aspect of the project takes place about a week after the conferences have been held. I hand out Figure 1 as a guide for the paper and go over it. Also, I give my students a reprint of one of my articles as a model for writing up their research although there are many articles available that would work just as well as mine. I use my (Lewis, 1989) study of the Heysel stadium soccer riot in Brussels Belgium as the model.

I also give a short lecture on techniques for overcoming writer's block. I point out that all writers block and that even Ernest Hemingway was a "sweater". I then take my students through the steps of getting over writer's block.

The first thing to do is to discuss your project with a friend. This friend should never be critical, but only supportive. After the discussion, write a narrative of how you explained your project to your friend. Second, write a letter to a friend describing your project, but don't send it. Make it the opening paragraphs of your essay.

Third, start a diary of your research project where you make daily entries. This narrative experience should help you get started. Fourth, write a letter to friend or loved one on any subject. This should prime the pump if all else has failed.

Reporting point 8. A week before the paper is due, students in class are asked to report on their work to date. This is where I ask each member to report the status of their project in terms of the writing. I call it the "draft status." I move around the class asking each to report the current progress of his or her research as well as the draft status of the paper. Of course, there is a great range of responses from "still researching" to "beginning to type the final draft." This often solicits groans from people who are not at this point in their work. Peer pressure is such that rarely does a student admit that he or she is finished with the paper.

FIGURE II
HANDOUT FOR CHECK LIST QUESTIONS

INTRODUCTION TO SOCIOLOGY
(Lewis)
SPRING, 1994

Here are some questions you should answer before you turn in your paper:

1.   Have I approached my research problem theoretically?

2.   Is the theoretical approach clearly explained in the paper?

3.   Have I approached the research problem using triangulation? Or have I made suggestions for using triangulation?

4.   Has the analysis reflected the theoretical model or models that were proposed? Did the analysis use a variety of data?

5.   Have I written this paper carefully? Have I had someone else read it? Did I use "Grammatik" or some other software to evaluate the paper?

6.   Was the bibliography annotated?

7.   Do I have a back up copy?

8.   Did I buy a nice folder for the paper (NO PLASTIC)?

BE SURE TO GET THE PAPER IN ON TIME

FIGURE III

<u>HANDOUT FOR TERM PAPER GRADE SHEET</u>

INTRODUCTION TO SOCIOLOGY
(LEWIS)
FALL, 1994

TERM PAPER GRADE SHEET

I. STUDENT NAME: ID:

II. PAPER TITLE:

III. THEORY (10): EXCELLENT GOOD FAIR POOR   ____

IV. METHODS/ANALYSIS (20): EXCELLENT GOOD FAIR POOR ____

V. WRITING: (10) EXCELLENT GOOD FAIR POOR   ____

                                        TOTAL POINTS:(40)   ____

COMMENTS:

                                        JERRY M. LEWIS
                                        PROFESSOR
                                        DEPARTMENT OF SOCIOLOGY

I hand out the sheets for the final aspects of preparing the paper as well as the grade sheet form (Figures II and III) and answer questions. The grade sheet (Figure III) generates the most questions. Of particular concern is the writing requirement which I try to explain stressing technical aspects of writing such as paragraph logic, grammar and spelling.

Reporting point 9. The last stage of the paper is handing it in. I do not have the students hand it in during a regular class period because I learned early on that a portion of the class will cut that day to work on last minute revisions. Thus, the paper is generally due on a Friday by 5 p.m. at my office. I try to be around during the afternoon as students turn in the paper because they often like to chat about their research and the problems they had with it. Mainly you listen to "war stories" that every researcher has experienced a dozen times, but it is important for the students to tell their professor about their experiences.

It gives students a better feeling about their projects if they do not just put the paper into a mailbox, but actually give it to the professor. Twenty percent or so of the students typically turn the paper in late so I have a procedure for dealing with late papers, but the student must inform me that the paper is going to be turned in late.

Student Responses to Projects

"BUT PROFESSOR LEWIS, THIS ISN'T SATTERFIELD HALL," responded a shocked student when I assigned the term paper on the first day of class, and announced that writing quality as well as ideas would be graded. (Satterfield Hall is the home of the English Department at Kent State University).

Students are fairly positive about the project. They tell me that it allows them to develop generalizable skills for doing projects in other courses. It is not so much the project topics per se that helps students but rather it is the act of carrying out the project and writing it up that is the growth experience. Of course, as is true of most teaching activities, there are joys and sorrows associated with the project. The joys lie in watching and helping a student take an original idea from scratch and build it into an acceptable project. One of my professors once told me that writing was a matter of confidence that you could carry a project to completion. Building confidence in one's students, particularly in relation to their writing, is a great joy.

Second, it allows me to encourage students to broaden their horizons. Sociology lies between the sciences and the humanities. In our teaching, sociologists have more flexibility to call on images from literature, art, music and dance to explain the social patterns and processes they are studying. For example, I often use the mosaic of Renoir's paintings to describe the structure of English soccer crowds. Ironically this sort of imagery is not usually available to me in my scientific writing particularly in professional sociology journals. However, one can use it when encouraging undergraduates to write. The irony is that I can urge my students to use imageries and analogies in discussing subjects in ways that I probably could not use in my own publishing efforts. It is fun to encourage them to take analytical risks.

There are sorrows. Two deserve mention. Some students come to my classes with such poor training in writing that it is difficult to really encourage them to do the project. You wonder why the educational system of which we are all part did not catch their weaknesses sooner. But you carry on.

This leads to the other sorrow. The project is very time consuming. Hence, it simply is not available to introductory courses with an enrollment greater than forty to fifty students.

Grading the Paper

The grade for the paper ranges from twenty to thirty per cent of my students total grade in the course.

The grades are traditional: excellent, good, average, and poor. I grade the paper on theory, analysis and writing. Within the category of writing, I divide the grading into two categories: mechanics and creativity.

By "mechanics," I refer to such things as spelling, grammar, logic and so forth. By "creativity," I mean using imagery that communicates what happened in the episode in such a way that the reader has a feeling of being present. Needless to say, the grading of the creativity part is much more subjective and difficult than the mechanics part.

Using Surveys or Secondary Data As Alternative Research Projects

There are two alternatives to the observational project. The first is to design an interview survey while the second is to do a secondary analysis of survey data. Although, I encourage students to do the observational study, some want to design survey. Most of the activity of the reporting points remains the same, except that I have an extra class, at another time, to show students how to move nominal questions to ordinal or interval measures.

A second alternative is to do secondary analysis of survey data. Many sociologists use the data sets available from NORC. Term projects using data sets are similar to studying the episode through field work. The teacher encourages students to develop hypotheses which are tested with empirical data. You follow the same teaching logic of reporting points for project, but focus is on secondary data analysis.

As an alternative to students working with the same data set, some publishers provide individual data sets where the students actually have their own disk with the data in tables and/or displayed graphically. The student follows the normal research process of developing a research question, formulating a theory, operationalizing propositions into hypotheses and analyzing the data. The advantage of computer programs is that the student does not have to collect his or her data. As all researchers know, things go wrong in data collection and the student does not have to be worried about these difficulties. Consequently, more time is spent on hypothesis formulation and testing with data analysis. Whenever you pick a textbook, you should investigate the computer and data programs the publisher has to offer. Students must have access to PCs to do these programs.

One question that always comes up when discussing the research project in the introductory course is how many students can you handle with this project. My own experience along with talking with other professors suggests the answer, as I noted earlier, is between forty and fifty students. This is true for two reasons. First, some students will have difficulty most of the way through the project. This begins with not knowing what topic to study to not being able to write up the project. You simply have to work with the student all through the project. The other type of student is one who is so excited about the project that she or he wants to share experiences every step of the way. While this is fun for the teacher, it takes time.

Sometimes students want to work together and do a team project. I generally agree to this because, after all, most social science research is collaborative. However, I warn the students that they must accept one grade on the project. I will not get into the business of referring who did more work than whom.

The next section of **TIPSTEACH** examines a variety of issues associated with course evaluations.

REFERENCES

Lewis, J. M. 1986. "A Protocol for the Comparative Analysis of Sports Crowd Violence". *International Journal of Mass Emergencies and Disasters*. 4:2 (August): 211-225.

Lewis, J. M. 1989. "A Value-Added Analysis of the Heysel Stadium Soccer Riot". *Current Psychology*. 8:1:15-29.

Shelly, R. K., Anderson, L, and Mattley, C. "Assembling Processes in A Periodic Gathering: Halloween in Athens, Ohio". *Sociological Focus*. 25:2 (May) 25:2: 139-150.

SECTION EIGHT
COURSE EVALUATIONS

Written with D. E. Benson

Introduction

The evaluation of teaching by students, peers and administrators is now a fixture of academic life. Since the turbulent 1960s, there has been increasing demand for the formal evaluation of teaching by administrators, legislators, parents and students. Peter Seldin (1993) reports that in a study of 600 liberal arts schools, the percentage using student evaluations has gone up from twenty-nine (29%) percent in 1973 to eighty-six (86%) percent in 1993. It is likely that other types of colleges and universities would report the same pattern.

Sometimes evaluations have been tied directly to classroom concerns. In other cases, however, they have been linked to ancillary issues such as student retention and public demands for more evaluation of classroom teaching and faculty accountability. These demands are becoming increasingly louder in the 1990s making this activity more important than in previous decades. This process can have very negative consequences. We have seen beginning introductory teachers both devastated by a few nasty evaluations as well as unduly elated by some good ones. In our view, neither response is appropriate. You should look at all of your evaluations as a "package." You cannot flee from the evaluation of teaching and you should not try to do so. We suggest you embrace the process and learn from it.

Depending on college or university policies, you will likely encounter a variety of formal evaluative procedures for your introductory teaching. Let's look at three major ones: student course evaluations, peer evaluations, and administrative evaluations.

Student Course Evaluations

This is the most prevalent form of evaluation used by most schools. It is usually based on a questionnaire-type instrument that is completed sometime in the final weeks of the term. There are both forced-choice and open-ended questions on the instrument with most questions being the former. Forced-choice are usually Likert-type with five to seven points ranging from "Strongly agree" to "strongly disagree." Be sure you understand the scoring of the instrument used at your school. A teaching assistant in our department hit the "panic button" when he got the results of his first evaluation and his scores were low. It was pointed out that the scoring used by Kent State means a low evaluation score (1's and 2's) indicates student perceptions of "good" teaching. As in the sport of cross country, a low score is a desirable score.

An instrument developed to measure students' evaluations of teaching can be used in a variety of ways. It can be used, idiosyncratically, by one department, by all departments in a particular college (eg., Arts and Science) or by the entire school. At Kent State, we use the same basic instrument for every department although each department is free to add its own questions.

There are five types of substantive questions typically used on student course evaluations. First, there are those that get at the actual mechanics of teaching. For example, questions such as "The instructor makes effective use of class time" or "The course was well organized", or "The instructor gave good examples." These questions measure skills that are directly involved with, and related to, the communication of information and are under the control of the instructor.

Second, there are questions related to course requirements. For example, whether the course has an appropriate number of evaluations or the syllabus has clearly stated the procedures that would be used to evaluate the work of students in the course. These questions measure an instructor's course from a technical, organizational perspective. These are things that can be developed by the instructor as a skill.

A third type of question attempts to measure interpersonal interaction between student and instructor. These include questions such as "The instructor shows respect for students." This type of question assesses the degree to which the instructor is courteous towards students and treats them with dignity and respect.

Fourth, there are questions about how course "outcomes" are perceived such as what grade the student expects from the course. Another might assess the amount of work required in the course vis-a-vis how much knowledge was acquired.

While the above types of questions attempt to assess specific aspects of the pedagogical situation, the fifth type of question is concerned with a "global" evaluation of course and/or instructor. Global questions are <u>very</u> important. They are often used in rehiring, tenure, promotion and merit decisions. There are several types of global questions. Most of the questions deal with course and instructor. For example, a global course question could be phrased, "Overall, the course was. . ." with a Likert-scale set of responses from "excellent" to "very poor." Similarly, the instructor question might read, "Overall, this instructor's teaching was. . ." with the responses ranging from "excellent" to "very poor." Another type of global question asks the student to compare this particular course with all other sociology courses the student has taken. For example, "In comparison with other sociology courses, I learned a great deal," with the response choices ranging from "Strongly agree" to "Strongly disagree". The instructor question is usually similar, "When compared with other sociology instructors, I learned a great deal," with choices of "Strongly agree" to "Strongly disagree" Finally, another type of global question, with similar response options, can be connected to the evaluative experience: "Considering the previous questions, how would you rate this professor (the course) in comparison to all others you have had?"

Almost all student evaluation instruments have a place for "open-ended" comments such as, "What aspects of this course were successful (need to be improved)?" or "Any comments about class management?" These qualitative sections can provide you with considerable insight and more detail about the undergraduate perceptions of your course. They also can be sources of humor as one of our colleagues reported when a student wrote, "Dr. _____, you are a great teacher but I still believe in Jesus" or in another case, a student commented, "Professor _____ is Dr. Jekyll and Mr. Hyde. He is funny in class, but not friendly in the office."

Stereotypes About Student Evaluations

There are many reasons why sociologists resist student course evaluations for assessing teaching performance. Most of these reasons are based on beliefs or "stereotypes" that faculty hold regarding teaching.

There are several stereotypes about student evaluations that one often hears among new instructors of introductory sociology. First, is the belief that it is impossible to get reliable or valid measures of student perceptions of teaching. This is because, it is argued, the teaching enterprise is too complex and idiosyncratic and, therefore, students cannot make solid, worthwhile judgments about courses and instructors. We find this a curious argument since sociologists are willing to study almost any topic dealing with social interaction and social groups irrespective of how complex or idiosyncratic it may be. Sociologists regularly study subjects where measurement is difficult, complex and demanding, e.g., family decision making, organizational change, soccer riots and the development of a self. Surely such topics are as complex and idiosyncratic as the evaluation of classroom teaching. We think it is possible to develop reliable and valid scales of student perceptions of teaching that will measure the important dimensions of the enterprise called classroom teaching (Benson and Lewis, 1993).

Further these scales can explain much of the variation in the scores for the global evaluation of instructors that are often used in personnel decisions.

Second, student evaluations are based on the popularity of the instructor. Those teaching assistants who do a great "soft shoe" are rewarded by students with high evaluations though the knowledge base from which they operate may be either archaic or absent. Therefore, those teachers who are not demanding will get high evaluations; those professors who are demanding of their students will receive lower student evaluation scores. This stereotype seems to be based on the very cynical assumption that students are only interested in being "entertained," and doing as little work as possible.

Third, the relationship between high grades in a course and the evaluation of the faculty member is positive and linear. That is, students who get good grades in a course will give a very positive evaluation of that course and the instructor who teaches it. In contrast, those who get lower grades do not give high evaluations to either course or instructor. Ironically, this belief appears to have a history in the literature on teaching evaluations. Borgatta and Bohrnstedt (1976) propose that the only way to evaluate a teacher is to have other referees grade papers. They write, "If actual learning is the criterion, the instructors [of sociology] should not grade their own papers or otherwise evaluate the students, since the instructors may vary in how they apply standards of grading." Beyond the practicality of these suggestions, this is a solution to a problem that may not exist.

Peter Seldin (1993) suggests there is no credible empirical evidence to support any of these stereotypes. Many researchers of this subject (e.g., Abrami 1989; Abrami et al. 1980; Abrami and d'Apollonia 1990; Abrami et al. 1990; Benson and Lewis 1993; Seldin 1993) also find these stereotypes to be false.

A Case Illustration

As an illustration of the above discussion, we analyzed the results of 3658 student evaluations of all courses given in the sociology department at Kent State for a given semester. The instrument is one used by all departments at Kent State University. Our first task was to determine the degree of validity and reliability possessed by the instrument. A standard technique for investigating the construct validity of a scale is exploratory, principle components factor analysis (Carmines and Zeller, 1979). Using the data set generated by the student evaluation instrument, we performed a principal components factor analysis, with varimax rotation, of all the items in the evaluation form (see Appendix for a list of the questions). This procedure resulted in isolating four factors with eigenvalues over unity. For an item to be included in any of the four factors, we used the **very** conservative standard of a loading of at least 0.50. Table 1 contains the items that comprise the factors, and their loadings.

TABLE 1

Items and Factor Loadings for the Student Evaluation Instrument

	Factor			
	1	2	3	4
1. Instructor used class time effectively	.8114			
2. Instructor gave clear explanations	.7910			
3. . . .summarized ideas effectively	.7650			
4. Course was well organized	.7719			
5. Examples and illustrations used well	.7119			
6. Instructor enthusiastic about subject	.5211			
7. Expected grade in the course		.6823		
8. How many classes did you miss		.6557		
9. Grade Point average at this time		.6333		
10. Amount of work I did for course		.5939		
11. Course requirements in syllabus			.7174	
12. Evaluation procedures in syllabus			.7062	
13. Course objectives in syllabus			.6761	
14. Appropriate number of evaluations			.6488	
15. Grading method was fair			.6142	
16. Students kept informed of progress			.5711	
17. Work load was appropriate			.5722	
18. Instructor showed respect for students				.7030
19. Instructor available for consultation				.6840
20. Instructor receptive to questions				.6791
21. Instructor stimulated thinking				.5528
Factor Name	TEACH	EXTERNAL*	MANAGE	PERSONAL
Cronbach Alpha	.912	.499	.879	.843

*Factor dropped from subsequent analysis.

The first factor is composed of six questions (items 1-6 on Table 1): effective use of class time, the instructor gave clear explanations , summarized ideas effectively , the course was well organized , used examples and illustrations well, and was enthusiastic about the subject. This factor explained 21.5% of the total variance.

Cronbach's alpha, a widely used technique to assess measurement reliability (Carmines and Zeller, 1979), was used to evaluate the degree to which the items comprising this factor were found to be internally consistent and, thus, a reliable measure of this factor. The alpha value for these six items was 0.912 indicating a very high degree of reliability (DeVellis 1991). Five of these six items (the exception being #1), clearly measure skills that are directly involved with the communication of information, are under the control of the instructor, and are talents that can be learned and taught. Taken as a group, these are items that almost anyone with a knowledge of pedagogy would define as being at the core of what it takes to be a good classroom teacher. We call this factor TEACH.

The third factor[1] we label MANAGE, and is made up of seven questions (11-17 on Table 1) including clear course requirements in the syllabus, whether the course has an appropriate number of evaluations, clearly stated evaluation procedures in the syllabus, fair grading method, students informed on their progress and appropriate workload for the course (#18). This factor explains 18.63% of the total variance with an alpha of 0.879. These items assess how well the instructor administers or manages the course. If the first factor is concerned with the content and its transmission to the students, this factor is concerned with the medium of the transmission and its "packaging." As with the items in the TEACH factor, all these administrative aspects can be learned and taught.

The fourth factor we label PERSONAL because the questions (items 18-21 on Table 1) included in this factor appear to be concerned with the quality of interpersonal relationships that exist between student and instructor. This factor includes four questions: instructor shows respect for students, is available for consultation, is receptive to questions and stimulates thinking. This factor explains 14.06% of the total variance with an alpha of 0.843. The first two questions seem to tap the sensitivity the instructor has toward his or her undergraduates. The last two questions also loaded, although less strongly, on the TEACH factor. This suggests that finding an instructor intellectually stimulating is a combination of pedagogical skills of the instructor and positive, sympathetic interaction between instructor and student.

---

[1] A second factor was dropped due to a low alpha score.

The combined three factors explain a robust 54.1% of the total variance indicating, as others have found (see above), that it is possible to develop valid and reliable scales that measure students' *perceptions* of the quality of undergraduate instruction using the same psychometric criteria that we would use to investigate any sociological phenomenon.

We next asked, "To what extent would these same factors help to explain the students' global evaluation of the instructor?" Table 2 presents the results of regression equations of the "overall evaluation of the instructor" on all three of the above identified factors: TEACH, MANAGE, and PERSONAL.

TABLE 2

Regression Equations of "Teach," "Manage," and "Personal" on the Overall Evaluation of the Instructor (standardized coefficients follow unstandardized in parentheses)

Variables		SE	T Value
Teach	0.1567 (0.6910)**	0.029	49.2057
Personal	0.0681 (0.1914)**	0.005	14.0213
Manage	0.0079 (0.0352)*	0.003	2.5990

$R = .868$

$R^2 = .753$

$N = 3292$
*$p < .01$
**$p < .0001$

By inspection, it can be seen in Table 2 that the three factors identified above through factor analysis, explain a robust 75% of the variance ($R^2 = 0.753$) in the students' overall evaluation of the instructor. Much of this explained variance is accounted for by the variable TEACH. These results suggest that the three factors identified in the factor analysis can explain, statistically, much of the variation in global evaluation scores for instructors. As others have found (see above), these data suggest that the first stereotype is incorrect.

Relative to the second stereotype discussed above, we performed a regression equation (not shown) on "amount of work I put into this course" (#3) and the global evaluation of the instructor. If this belief is correct, this variable should explain a considerable amount of the variation in the global evaluative measure. Instead the item explained only about 2.5% of the variance ($R^2 = 0.026$) indicating virtually no relationship between these two variables. We performed a similar analysis on the item "the grade I expect in this course is:__," and the global evaluation of the instructor (the third stereotype discussed above). As with the second stereotype the regression equation (not shown), indicates that this variable explains just over 2% of the variance ($R^2 = 0.021$). Again, we conclude that these data do not support this stereotype.

As others have found (see above) this case illustration demonstrates that the quantitative evaluation of classroom teaching is amenable to the same type of analysis that sociologists use to investigate other interactional phenomenon. It also indicates that some of the stereotypes held by academics to thwart the evaluation of classroom teaching are largely unfounded. These data do not measure the relationship between how much a student *actually* learns in a course and the quality of classroom instruction. They do suggest, however, that a psychometrically sound instrument can assess students' perceptions of classroom teaching.

Peer Evaluations

The next type of classroom teaching evaluation you are likely to encounter is peer evaluation. This type of evaluation usually occurs at crucial points in a teacher's career such as promotion or tenure but can come more often depending on the policies of the college or university. A peer evaluation means that one of your colleagues comes to your class to evaluate your teaching. Usually it is one class, but it can be more. When a tenure decision is involved, this type of evaluation involve more than one peer. The visitor usually critiques the class on several factors, and writes a report that is submitted to the instructor being evaluated. This evaluation becomes part of his or her permanent record.

These visits can be very instructive but they can also be nerve-racking. We would recommend you have a "friendly peer" evaluate your class before the official evaluation is conducted.

While it is unusual for graduate students to be formally evaluated by peers, there is nothing wrong with asking another graduate student to sit in on your class for an evaluation. You might also want to sit in on classes of more experienced graduate students for some insights into how they teach the class or a particular subject.

Administrative Evaluation

Administrative evaluation is rarer than student or peer evaluation but such evaluation does occur. This type of evaluation will probably increase in the future as the concern with evaluating teaching intensifies. Administrative evaluators are usually chairpersons who may be from within or outside the department. With teaching assistants, the director of graduate or undergraduate education in a department or both will probably do the evaluation. Rarely is there an administrative evaluation of teaching assistants or part-time instructors from outside the department. The administrative evaluation is similar to the peer evaluation except that this person represents the interests and perspectives of the entire department. Generally, the administrative evaluator writes a report of the teacher which then becomes part of his or her personnel file. The teacher is usually given a copy of these reports. These evaluations can be used with graduate students and part-time teachers for reappointment and/or rehiring decisions. For tenure track professors, they are part of the personnel file and are used in all important career decisions such as tenure, promotion, and merit.

The Classroom Visit

The administrative visit to the classroom can be threatening for any instructor whether he or she is an old "pro" or a beginning teacher. This part of **TIPSTEACH** will try to give an "ideal-typical" sense of what is occurring when your teaching is administratively evaluated. The actual form of the administrative evaluation will vary from department to department depending on department and university policies.

You are likely to be evaluated by a visit to your classroom late in the quarter or semester. The evaluator will contact you about the evaluation and work out an appropriate time for the evaluation. It is rare that the evaluator will appear "unannounced" for an evaluation. Typically, the evaluator will ask you for your course syllabus, or secure one from the department before coming to your class.

On the appointed day, the evaluator will come to class and usually sit in the back of the room. You may wish to introduce the evaluator to the class to prevent your students from spending time trying to identify the function and purpose of this "stranger" in the back of the room.

While it is very difficult, try not to "teach to the evaluator." To aid you in this goal, it is a good idea to have a peer evaluation before an administrative evaluation so you can adjust to having a "foreigner" in your class.

The evaluator will likely take notes throughout the class. One senior person we know who does many evaluations, takes two types of notes throughout the class. One set are "content" notes that any student would be writing down while the other are "teaching" notes. Needless to say, this type of evaluator writes a great deal and frequently is writing when students are just listening.

At the end of the class, the evaluator may talk briefly with students or schedule an appointment to talk with the students. These interviews will likely be included in the evaluation report.

Evaluation Criteria

What will the evaluator be looking for in his or her visit to your class? In evaluating any class, administrative evaluators tend to use four criteria. These are preparation, enthusiasm, linkage to the discipline and respect for students.

Preparation is first assessed from the syllabus. The evaluator notes whether students know what is expected that day. For example, if the topic for the day is the religious institution, is there appropriate assigned material for this topic? Second, does the instructor clearly express what he or she intends to accomplish in the class?   This is done in a variety of ways. Many instructors write the day's agenda on the board and may discuss it with the class. Alternatively, some instructors will hand out a written agenda with definitions and discussion questions on it. Last, it is possible to set the agenda for the day's work by reviewing the previous class and asking for questions about the work.

A third indicator of preparation is whether the instructor ends the lecture with a summary of the information presented that day and set of questions or ideas for the next lecture discussion group. Most teachers have no trouble initiating class but some have difficulty ending it. Adequate preparation means that you are prepared, you are in control of your material and the time allotted for presenting it. A good summary with some transition questions at the end will give your students closure on the lecture.

Enthusiasm is a difficult factor to evaluate, but most administrative evaluations try to assess it in some fashion. One way is to survey student interest in the class before the class begins. One can ask: "Are you looking forward to the class?" Are undergraduates talking about the assignment or the day's work before the professor arrives? In many ways this is the best accolade an introductory professor could receive.

Another measure of enthusiasm is the professor's own greeting to students. The first few minutes of any class are very important. If you are glad to be there and excited about the day's work, share this with your students. Your enthusiasm will be transmitted to your students. We had colleague who told us that if he was not excited about a class, he would run up and down stairs to get motivated for his class. Another colleague vocalizes like an opera singer before a class. Both are warming up in the same way as an athlete would prepare for a game or match.

The linkage of the course to the discipline of sociology is another factor on which you may be evaluated. The ASA report (1991) on liberal learning, strongly suggests that the introductory course should be linked to the discipline of sociology. Lewis' research on outstanding teachers suggests that they are very involved with their particular discipline. In the introductory course, you cannot be expected to be training your introductory students to be sociologists. You will be expected to apply the ideas of the course in a way that reflects the disciplinary approach to intellectual questions to life in society.

Finally, you are likely to be evaluated in terms of your respect for students. This can be shown in many ways. The teacher can go to considerable effort to draw students into class discussions. This is often done through humor, appreciation of previous participation, or direct invitations to participate. Typically, the administrative evaluator will try to estimate what percentage of the class participated in discussion. Of course, the quality of participation is often related to the size and type of class.

After the class visit is completed, the evaluator will probably discuss the evaluation with you in an informal way. This is not a required procedure but it is common to do so. The evaluator writes a report on your class and submits it to the chair of the department and/or the director of undergraduate teaching and it is placed into your personnel file. You are entitled to see the final report and the chair of the department will probably discuss it with you.

The Consequences of Evaluations

Your first reaction to the fact that your teaching is going to be evaluated will likely be negative. Your responses are likely to follow two lines of thought. First, there is the "bad day" response. The argument is that most teachers of the introductory course are, by training and intellect, good teachers but are prone to "off" or "bad days" on occasion (or semesters, years, or careers). Therefore, what happens if the evaluator has caught the teacher on a "bad day?" In most departments, if your perception is that it was a "bad day," you can ask the evaluator to reschedule the class visit for another time. Most departments want to see you at your best.

Second, there is the "pornography" problem; paraphrasing American Supreme Court Justice Potter Stewart who said, "I can't define pornography but I know it when I see it." This belief argues that it is difficult to define (and study) outstanding teaching, but easy to recognize it (not unlike the above discussion). You can legitimately ask, "Is the evaluator who comes to my class, knowledgeable and fair in evaluating teaching?" Without being too much of a Pollyanna, most of the evaluators who come to your class are primarily interested in helping you become a better introductory teacher.

After you recover from, or at least manage, the negative feelings about the class visits, you have to deal with the results of the evaluative procedures. Typically you will receive the course evaluations in the term following the course that was evaluated. Our experience suggests that you will probably look for the negative aspects of the evaluations first and then positive responses - whether quantitative or qualitative. Students' evaluations are usually returned in a statistical format which allows you to compare your evaluations with comparable courses taught by others. Included in this package, will be the qualitative evaluations in raw form or summarized. You are likely to be stung by negative comments - and they will be there. No matter how hard you try and how terrific you are as a teacher, some students will not like what you did. After you recover from the initial shock of the evaluations, we recommend that you go to an experienced, trusted faculty member in the department and discuss the quantitative and qualitative aspects of the student evaluations. Explore with this colleague what can be done to improve your course and its evaluations. You may also want to go to the chair of the department for this discussion.

Embracing the Evaluation Experience

Instead of fleeing from the evaluation experience, we propose that you welcome it. Goldsmid and Wilson (1980: p. 334) succinctly tell us, "There are at least four reasons for systematic appraisals of instructor performance: instructors need them, students need them, administrators need them and life itself requires them." That "life requires them" points to the inevitability of evaluation. Your course and your teaching are being evaluated daily by your students. You should accept this and try to learn from the experience and the outcome. We recommend that you do some analysis of your evaluations along the lines suggested in the case history.

McKeachie (1978) and Seldin (1993) tell us the conditions that encourage the use of student evaluation to improve teaching. First, the evaluations should provide new information. The quantitative distributions and qualitative data should provide information of which you were not aware. If the instructor realizes the data are showing a new problem about some aspect of the teaching, he or she is likely to try to develop some solutions. You need to carefully study you evaluations and compare them with past semesters. Some schools also provide norming groups for sections of other introductory courses.

Second, the instructor must be motivated to improve. We are not sure what we can say here other than, "Win one for the Gipper." If you are reading the eighth section of a monograph on teaching the introductory course you are probably already motivated to teach well.

Third, the teacher must know how to change. There is no substitute for talking with peers and colleagues about your teaching successes and failures. Once you receive your evaluations and have studied them, have trusted peers and colleagues review your data. They can help by pinpointing areas that might be improved. Next, develop a plan for improving your teaching and put it into effect in the next semester. See if these changes improve your evaluations. We think they will.

Some universities have faculty development centers and such units are likely to increase in the coming years. If your college or university has one, visit it and see how the staff can help you carry out your teaching improvement plan.

In the next section of **TIPSTEACH** is an examination of subject appropriately following student evaluations - using humor in the classroom.

REFERENCES

American Sociological Association. 1991. *Liberal Learning and the Sociology Major*. Washington, D.C.

Abrami, P.C., Dickens, W.J., Perry, R.P. and Leventhal, L. 1980. "Do Teacher Standards for Assigning Grades Affect Student Evaluation of Instruction?" *Journal of Educational Psychology*, 72, 107-118.

Abrami, P.C. 1989. "How Should We Use Student Ratings To Evaluate Teaching?" *Research In Higher Education* 30:221-227.

Abrami, Philip C., d'Apollonia, S. and Cohen, P. A. 1990."Validity of Student Ratings of Instruction: What We Know and What We Do Not," *Journal of Educational Psychology* 82:219-231.

Abrami, P.C., and d'Apollonia, S. 1990. "The Dimensionality of Ratings and Their Use in Personnel Decisions," Pp. 97-111 in M. Theall and J. Franklin, (Eds.) *Student Ratings of Instruction: Issues For Improving Practice*. San Francisco: Jossey-Bass.

Benson, D. and Lewis, J. M. 1993. "Student Evaluation of Teaching and Accountability: Implications from the Boyer and ASA Reports." *Teaching Sociology*. Forthcoming.

Borgatta, Edgar F. and Bohrnstedt, G. W. 1976. "Some Outrageous Consequences of Valid Teacher Ratings" *Social Science*, 51 (#2):69-75.

Boyer, E. 1990. *Scholarship Reconsidered: Priorities of the Professoriate*. Princeton, N.J.: The Carnegie Foundation.

Callahan, J.P. 1992. "Faculty Attitude Towards Student Evaluation" *College Student Journal*, 26, 98-102

Carmines, E.G., and Zeller, R.A. 1980. *Reliability and Validity Assessment*. Beverly Hills: Sage.

Cohen, P. 1981. "Student Ratings of Instruction and Student Achievement: A Meta-Analysis of Multisection Validity Studies" *Review of Educational Research*, 51, 281-309.

DeVellis, R.F., 1991. *Scale Development: Theory and Applications*. Beverly Hills:Sage.

Feldman, K. A. 1989. "The Association Between Student Ratings of Specific Instructional Dimensions and Student Achievement: Refining and Extending the Synthesis of Data from Multisection Validity Studies," *Research in Higher Education* 30, 583-645.

Goldsmid, C. A., and Wilson, E. K. 1980. *Passing on Sociology: The Teaching of a Discipline*. Belmont, CA: Wadsworth.

Kohlan, Richard. 1973. "A Comparison of Faculty Evaluations Early and Late in the Course," *Journal of Higher Education*. 44:8; 587-595.

McKeachie, W. J. 1978. *Teaching Tips*. Seventh Edition. Lexington, Mass.: D. C. Heath.

Seldin, Peter. 1991. *The Teaching Portfolio*. Bolton, MA: Anker   Publishing Company.

Seldin, Peter. 1993. "The Use and Abuse of Student Ratings of Professors" *The Chronicle of Higher Education* 7/21/93, p. A-40.

SECTION NINE
HUMOR IN THE CLASSROOM

Introduction

Dealing with course evaluations may encourage you to turn to humor. Humor crops up in our students interpersonal relationships and our own. Sociologists should help introductory students make sense of the humor of everyday life. This section begins with a discussion of the pervasiveness of humor. It moves to an analysis of how award winning teachers use humor. The section concludes with case history illustrating using humor in teaching occupational socialization.

The Pervasiveness of Humor

Humor is everywhere in our culture. Politicians use it; business people use it; and church leaders use it. Why can't sociologists who teach the introductory course use humor? They can and here is why.

On any given day we run into people who kid us, tell us a joke, give us a cartoon, or crack a snappy one liner. As a litmus test of this, think about the number of times between breakfast and lunch someone attempts to talk with you through some form of humor. We also use humor to find out about ourselves. How often do we do something that we decide is inappropriate, stupid, silly or just dumb and respond to it with a joke? Literally, we kid ourselves. One way to handle mistakes in a lecture is with a light one liner. When we mention the wrong page when discussing something in our introductory text, students quickly note our mistakes. It is easy, and not inappropriate to respond, "Just checking to see if you were paying attention."

A LITERACY OF HUMOR

I do not wish to elevate a literacy of humor to the level of importance of the ability to read print. As a teacher, I value and cherish the printed word. I wish to suggest a useful analogy between print and humor literacy.

How can we help our introductory sociology students develop a literacy of humor? How can we help them undertake the task of comprehending humor in American society? May I propose three principles for looking at humor. They are the principles of perspective, understanding, and norm, or PUN.

The first principle is **perspective**. In understanding the humor in American culture we should look for the perspective that is being communicated by the humor being used. Does the humorous message warn of a perspective of anger, fear, sadness, happiness, joy or a combination of emotions?

Second, humor suggests the level of **understanding** the joke teller is bringing to the situation. The humor presented can show the level of the speaker's information and thinking about problem or situation.

Third, humor reminds us of the **norms** the individual is bringing to a situation. These norms may not always be clear. A joke or witty remark can provide a clue to the norms that will guide the joke teller's behavior. In a sense a joke can be an announcement of what is going to happen next. Our introductory students probably can read the humor that surrounds them.

Humor Literacy and Abraham Lincoln

Let me illustrate, using the principles of PUN and an Abraham Lincoln story, how we can teach our students to understand the humor of a social situation.

A few United States presidents have used humor effectively. Some witty presidents have been Theodore Roosevelt, Harry S. Truman, John Kennedy, and Bill Clinton. But probably the most effective humorist was Abraham Lincoln. Lincoln's use of humor in political life moved through several stages. (Dunning, 1942.) At the beginning of his political career he used jokes and tall stories to ridicule opponents' ideas. After he became president, he used humor as a way of saying "No." Finally, with the responsibilities of the Civil War becoming so unbearable, he used humor as a way to lighten his burdens. Lincoln's use of humor can be understood with PUN and his presentation of the Emancipation Proclamation (1862) to his cabinet.

After Lincoln had informed his Cabinet of his plan for the Proclamation, one after another of the cabinet members spoke saying they liked this phrase or that but also had an objection or two. Lincoln (Jennison, 1988.) said to his cabinet:

> Gentlemen, this reminds me of the story of the man who had been away from home, and when he was coming back was met by one of his farm hands, who greeted him after this fashion: "Master, the little pigs are dead and the old sow's dead, too, but I didn't like to tell you all at once."

From this story the cabinet members understood that President Lincoln's **perspective** on Emancipation was very serious - as was the giving of very bad news a serious thing for the farm hand. The story shows that Lincoln **understood** that the cabinet members realized that the Proclamation was going to have great impact on American society - as the loss of the hogs had on the farmer. Lastly, the **norm** of behavior that Lincoln suggested was that he wanted his cabinet to know that he was going to be careful how he presented the Emancipation Proclamation to the American people. That he, too, "didn't like to tell you all at once." Historians may disagree with my interpretation, but I hope you will find the ideas of PUN useful in helping your introductory students think about humor.

Literacy of Humor

To be literate means to be able to read *and write*. I have been arguing that in the introductory course, the sociologist should attempt to make his or her students aware of the humor in society and how it is used. I have been writing about the "reading" aspects of literacy. There is another side of literacy of humor - that is the ability of the sociology instructor to "write" by communicating through humor. To get you thinking about your own use of humor, let me briefly share my own taste in humor. I particularly enjoy reading aphorisms which are short sayings stating a general truth that one often sees on professors' doors or in their offices. For example,

On Marriage:

"There is no record of any man being shot by his wife while he was washing dishes."

On College Teachers:

"A Professor is one who talks in someone else's sleep."

On Hard Work:

"He who cuts his own wood warms himself twice."   (Thoreau)

The Use of Humor in Introductory Teaching

Before you go running out the room saying, "Oh I can't tell jokes" or "I can never remember punch lines," let me say there is help available. It can be found in the styles of outstanding teachers, in the work of the stand up comedians and in David Adams (1992) manual on humor in the classroom.

Classroom Humor of Award Winning Professors

In my research on award winning professors (Lewis, 1993), I learned that these professors make considerable use of humor. I found that they used it in a variety of ways which can be summarized in the following typology.

FIGURE 1
TYPOLOGY OF HUMOR
PLANNING

	ANTICIPATED	UNANTICIPATED
YES	I	II
SUBJECT RELATED:		
NO	III	IV

The situational variable ranges from planned to spontaneous humor. A planned act of humor is one that the teacher anticipates using at a specific time in the course. It can range from a cartoon on an overhead to a long joke. In contrast, an unanticipated and spontaneous act of humor occurs at anytime in the class. It can range from a witty remark based on a student comment to a messed up experiment in chemistry class.

There is the contextual variable which relates to the subject of the course. The acts of humor are directly related to the subject of the class or not directly related. For example, a professor might want to illustrate a point in the lecture with a joke or cartoon. Many authors of introductory sociology textbooks use humor to illustrate their points. One of the best examples is a Gary Larson cartoon which shows a group of eels at a party with the caption reading, "Social Morays." (See Jon Shepard, *Sociology*, 1993, p. 84.) I showed this cartoon when I lecture on values and norms. In contrast, some professors like to use humor which is not necessarily related to the topic of the course.

The vast majority of humor falls into Type I, although instances of Type II's and III's were reported in my interviews with the outstanding teachers. Here are examples of Type I.

English Professor: "I will pun. That's the limit of my intellectual ability to create humor is the pun. And they are usually very terrible. I will frequently lighten a situation."

Geology Professor: "I think the most humorous thing I did was tell stories, often on myself, about a geological situation. (I slipped) off the edge of the cliff and fell 40 feet."

But the Psychology Professor is often a type III in his use of humor: "One liners. I guess if I could, I would be Johnny Carson sometimes. I would like to be one of those stand up comedians . . . " Another professor, a sociologist, begins almost every lecture with a joke which may be Type I, but often is not related to the course (Type III) subject matter.

The Stand-Up Comedian. Marshall McLuhan, the popular cultural theorist of the 1960s and 1970s, who is increasingly recognized as a post modern theorist, coined the phrase, the "medium is the message" (McLuhan, 1964). McLuhan wrote perceptively on the artist in modern life. He argued the importance of the artist to society. He said that it was the artist who tells us where society is and where it is going. The stand up comedian is an artist that we should pay attention to for social insight as well as a source of skills for communicating with humor. The stand up comedian or comedienne can provide great insight into the humor of our interpersonal relationships. This is true for several reasons. One, the stand up comic spends considerable time observing social relationships, thinking about them, and exaggerating them for humorous purposes. Thus, comprehending humor calls for us to pay serious attention to the work of Robin Williams, Richard Pryor, and/or Rita Rudner. Most sociology teachers have their favorite comedians. Here are some of mine.

Will Rogers on elections:

> Politics has got so expensive that it takes lots of money to even get beat with.

Woody Allen on speed reading:

> I took a speed reading course and I quickly read *War and Peace*. It was about a man visiting his sister.

A Manual on Humor

David Adams (1992) has developed a manual for using humor in the classroom that is available through the ASA's Teaching Resource Center. The manual is divided into three parts. First, there is an introductory essay by Adams which proposes some ideas for using humor based on empirical research (more on this shortly). Second, there is a category of humorous items that can be used for teaching various aspects of sociology. For example, under the category "family," there is a range of items that could be used to teach such subjects as kinship, sex, romantic love, or marital communication (Adams, 1992, pp. 36-39). Third, there is a useful bibliography of research on the use of humor in the classroom.

On the basis of a literature review on using humor, Adams (1992: pp.14-15) developed principles for using humor in the classroom. Adams' principles are for any level of teaching. I have considerably modified them for use in the introductory course.

Principle one - Use humor for openers. In any introductory sociology course there is an assortment of opening situations. The beginning of the course, the start of a class and the first few minutes of a test are good examples. All are times when humor can be used. For example, at the start of the course you can ask your students to name and describe their high school mascot. You can give a prize for the most unusual or the largest animal. The prize might be a candy bar or some type of representation of your college or university mascot.

Principle two - Use humor for transitions. There are many transitions in an introductory course. For example, from one   topic to another, from a quiz to a lecture and vice versa, from multiple choice questions to essay. All these "rites of passage could be times for a quick bit of humor. For example, after discussing kinship terminology, you might say, "now I want to discuss the typical American family" putting up a transparency of the Cleaver family from "Leave it to Beaver" or a picture of the Kennedys. You have to trust your judgment about what you think is funny. Anyway, the class responses will soon let you know.

Principle three - Encourage students to use humor. This is a very valuable idea. For, in using humor, students can begin to understand the humor that surrounds them. There are several ways that students can use humor. They can bring in cartoons that illustrate sociological ideas. They write down or even photograph silly signs in shopping malls. One of the silliest is, "Ears pierced while you wait." I have students take a serious diagram in an introductory sociology text and treat it as a cartoon. I asked them to work in groups writing a caption for the "cartoon." It works well. Students had fun and got some insight into the subject of the diagram (See exercise 27, p. 80).

Another time I asked students to draw a cartoon illustrating some idea associated with social roles. I said I wouldn't grade the art. A few of my students drew such wonderful cartoons that I used some of them, with the students' permission, in subsequent classes.

The previous principles have shown how humor can be used in teaching. But, using humor in teaching the introductory course is not without risks. David Adams' last two principles suggest ways that this risk can be reduced.

Principle four - Use relevant material. Adams comments that the audience must understand the joke, particularly when using satire. We professors like to pun which can be fraught with danger if one is too subtle. Sociologists are often described as having dry senses of humor which may be a polite word for being dull. I hope not. Anyway a dry sense of humor may serve to "WHET" student appetites for learning. (Sorry, I couldn't resist).

Principle five - Avoid humor that insults or ridicules students. Probably the best humor is self-deprecating humor. Since I have been teaching at Kent State a long time, I have had many photographs taken which I will show to introductory students. Recently, during an opening class, I asked jokingly if any students had parents who had me in class. This time the answer was yes, and my obvious surprise generated a good laugh among the students.

The campus newspaper can be a source of humor using cartoons or advertisements. Showing the cartoons or reading the advertisements can be great fun in class and a chance to look at the campus culture.

Illustrations of Adams' Principles Using a Case History

I use humor, in a variety of classroom situations, with a technique I call "Dr. J's Flea Market." I will first present the technique and then analyze it using Adams' principles.

I have developed a procedure called "Dr. J's flea market" that serves as both an icebreaker and a way to generate questions. I get a collection of items from garage sales and flea markets including mugs, glasses, baskets, cheap novels and holiday items. In the opening class you can use the flea market as an icebreaker. One way to get your introductory class students acquainted with each other is by asking nonthreatening demographic questions such as: "What student has a hometown that is the farthest or closest from campus?" "What students have 'devil' as a high school mascot?" You can come back to these questions in your religion lectures. Another question: "How many students have had sociology?" You can use the flea market idea to find out if any of the students come from foreign countries or have traveled abroad recently. Often you pick up souvenir mugs from other countries and you can ask, based on the mug, e.g. "In what French city is the Louvre located?" After each answer you give the respondent a flea market prize making sure that every participant gets something.

The second way to use the flea market idea goes beyond openers. It is a way to get students to "bid" on items by asking good questions anytime in the course. I judge the questions on the basis of imagination and insight into the social processes being studied. For example, if the question is, "What is the difference between a folkway and a more" then students get a low level flea market prize - say a basket or a cheap novel. If they ask using sociological ideas such as asking whether a campus newspaper is approaching an issue from functional or conflict perspectives, then the flea market item is worth more. It might be two baskets or a "better" mug. Students can ask questions from the floor or give them to me in writing before class.

I usually give precedence to questions from the floor, but everybody who asks gets a flea market item. Frequently I answer the questions immediately and award the prize. Occasionally, mostly involving policy issues and sociological analysis, I award the flea market prize but defer the answer to a later date so I can think about the question.

My course evaluations suggest that students enjoy the fun of the flea market even in large classes. I should note that I also used the technique as an icebreaker in upper divisions classes.

Adams' Principles and Dr. J's Flea Market

I want to conclude this section by using David Adams' principles for interpreting how I taught this case. This may be useful for your own use of humor in your introductory classes.

Regarding principle one, I **open** several lectures using the flea market. Sometimes it is as an icebreaker, while at other times it is designed to get students to ask questions. In a few of my classes, I have extended role plays. In those classes I give the participants in the role plays an item from the flea market.

For a **transition** (principle two), I use the flea market items to generate questions about the section just completed or the one that is about to begin.

In encouraging students to use humor (principle three), I will sometimes ask students to bring a cartoon to class germane to the subject under consideration. The funniest ones will win flea market items. The judging of the funniest is left to the instructor.

I made the flea market activities and its related humor **relevant** (principal four) to my students by always tying it into the course materials or activities. For example, to encourage students to look through the entire test before taking it. I autograph an interior page of one question booklet and the winner gets candy or a flea market item.

Lastly, the flea market does not **ridicule** students (principle five) because, for the most part, it is the items themselves that are a source of ridicule.

In the next section, of **TIPSTEACH**, I review the external resources available to help teach the introductory course.

REFERENCES

Adams, D. S. 1992. *Using Humor in Teaching Sociology: A Handbook*. Washington, DC.: ASA Teaching Resources Center.

Dunning, L. (ed) 1942. *Mr. Lincoln's Funnybone*. Howell Soskin.

Jennison, K. W. 1988. *The Humorous Mr. Lincoln*. Woodstock, Vermont: The Countryman Press.

Lewis, J. M. 1993. "Teaching Styles of Award-Winning Teachers" in R. Ellis, (ed.) *Quality Assurance for University Teaching*. Bristol, England: Open University Press. pp. 149-164.

Shepard, J. 1993. *Sociology* Fifth Edition. Minneapolis/St. Paul: West.

SECTION TEN
EXTERNAL SOURCES OF HELP

Introduction

I call this section of TIPSTEACH "External" to get across to you the idea that you are not alone when teaching the introductory course. As sociologists, I think we can be proud of the efforts of our discipline to develop quality undergraduate teaching. I deal with several sources of help in this section including book representatives, the ASA, *Teaching Sociology*, the national and regional sociology meetings, and help for teaching the mass class.

Book Representatives

Book representatives (or reps) are people who work for publishers whose job it is to convince you to adopt their textbooks for your courses. They typically call on you early in the semester or the quarter just to get acquainted with you and to learn what you teach and how you approach your courses. They are particularly interested in the introductory course since that is the big seller in textbooks. Rarely are book reps sociologists or even social scientists. Typically their college majors are in English, the humanities or business. Consequently, their knowledge of technical sociology will be limited. However, it is not for technical help that you draw on the services of the book rep.

There are three ways that the rep can support your teaching of the introductory course. First, the rep can provide you sample copies of the textbook, study guide, test banks and ancillary materials that the publisher has developed to support the textbook. In recent years, publishers have become quite imaginative in their development of ancillary materials. For example, it is possible to get a variety of such items as overheads, videos, all types of test banks and data analysis systems. Be sure you take time to discuss the things that are available from a publisher to support that textbook.

Second, the book rep can provide you with examples of how professors in your departments or other departments have used the publisher's materials in creative ways. For example, one publisher provided a supplement based on the *New York Times*. I developed a handout using the supplement which the book rep found interesting and shared with other professors of sociology in her territory.

Third, the rep can help you with problems when you do adopt a book from her publisher. Sometimes books do not show up in time for the start of the semester or quarter. (You should always check on the status of your textbook two or three weeks before school begins). A quick telephone call to the book rep can usually solve the problem. It is much easier to call a rep than to deal with publisher bureaucracies in New York City or Boston.

The American Sociological Association

The American Sociological Association (ASA) has done a great deal to help teaching in sociology including the introductory course. The ASA was founded in 1905 and represents sociology at the national and international levels. Headquartered in Washington, D.C., the ASA provides many services to its members including support for teaching. The activities of the ASA regarding teaching are quite varied. I will discuss three topics including handbooks, workshops, and the Teaching Resources Group.

Handbooks

ASA, through its Teaching Resources Center, develops handbooks and manuals to support teaching. There are over 75 handbooks available to the teacher. There are three types of handbooks. First, there are ones that focus on a particular subject such as collective behavior or religion. Second, there are handbooks that look at particular kinds of classes such as the mass class. Lastly, there are handbooks or manuals that focus on particular processes that happen in class such as assessment or using humor in teaching.

A very useful type of handbook related to particular subjects is one that contains syllabi. I have developed a new course without checking with ASA about the availability of a handbook, with syllabi, related to the course. For example, the handbook on the introductory course has fifteen syllabi in it. Besides handbooks, the ASA has other publications that are useful for teaching. The ASA at 1722 N. Street, N.W., Washington, D.C. 20036 will provide you a complete list of publications available through its Teaching Resources Center.

Workshops

Workshops are sponsored by the American Sociological Association (ASA) using staff drawn from sociologists with expertise in the subject matter of the workshop. The workshops are held periodically through the year as well as in connection with the ASA national meetings.

Workshop size is small, ranging, in my experience, from 20 to 50 participants, thus allowing for considerable interaction and sharing of ideas.

Workshops held away from the annual meetings tend to be on college campuses and usually charge fees. The activities of the workshop tend to follow the same general pattern. After presentations from the staff, students move into small group discussions with the results of being shared with the entire workshop. Often, there is time allowed for participants to think and write problems related to their own college or university. Sometimes this can be done in connection with individual contact with the staff.

Workshops at the annual ASA meetings are generally two hours long and are open to all registrants without additional charges. They are quite popular so plan to arrive early for programs. Here is a sample of some of the workshop titles for ones held at the ASA meetings in Miami Beach in 1993.
1.   Teaching the Sociology of Formal Organizations
2.   Teaching the Sociology of Religion
3.   Teaching the Sociology of Children
4.   Teaching Writing within the Sociology Curriculum
5.   Teaching Introductory Sociology For the First Time

Teaching Resources Group

The TRG is a group of scholars who have a strong commitment to teaching as well as a desire to support colleagues in their teaching activities. Their expertises range across all types of teaching environments from mass introductory courses to small graduate seminars. The TRG also represents the vast variety of substantive teaching areas in sociology. The members of the TRG meet annually at the national meetings. To draw on the support of the TRG you should contact the Teaching Services Program of the ASA.

Teaching Sociology

Teaching Sociology is a journal, sponsored by the ASA, devoted to the subject of sociology teaching. It is a quarterly journal that is available to you as a subscription choice if you join the ASA. Many libraries subscribe to it. It is likely that one or more of your colleagues will have subscriptions to *Teaching Sociology*.

Teaching Sociology has three basic types of articles which can be illustrated with material from a special issue of *Teaching Sociology* called "Gifts." The word "Gifts" refers to Great Ideas for Teaching Sociology.   First, there are empirical articles in the traditional sense of sociological analysis. For example, Hong (1992) shows how to use data to teach the ecological fallacy. Some empirical articles describe the culture of teaching in sociology such as how textbooks cover certain topics.

Second, there are articles out now on how a technique could be used in most any course. For example, Fisher (1992) writes about the use of films to attack stereotypes.

Third, there are articles that look at some teaching technique germane to a particular substantive area. For example, in the "Gifts" special issue Levy (1992) writes about how to teach ritual in a family course. This is the good news. There are a variety of articles that are helpful to you in teaching. The bad news is that there have been few articles on teaching the introductory course *per se* in the history of *Teaching Sociology*. Perhaps the future editors might devote a special issue to this topic. However, not all is lost. It is quite easy to adopt some general techniques to the introductory course. You might also consider submitting an article to *Teaching Sociology*, although, be fair warned, reviewing and editing are rigorous.

There are other journals not strictly related to the sociology discipline that might be helpful to you in your introductory teaching. Cashin and Clegg (1994) list seventy-six different academic disciples ranging from "Accounting" to "Women's Education" that have journals devoted to teaching. All the social sciences are present on the list. In addition, they present forty-seven higher education newspapers and journals that have articles on teaching. For example, they list *The Chronicle of Higher Education* as a source of articles on college teaching. Another good source is *College Teaching* which some of your colleagues may know by its former title of *Improving College and University Teaching*. *College Teaching* is a quarterly journal focusing on undergraduate and graduate teaching in all disciplines. Most of the articles, while discipline based, are designed to be used in a variety of teaching situations. For example, the Winter, 1993 issue had three articles on teaching writing in geography, marketing and English. If you are interested in getting ideas of some teaching process, I suggest you consult *College Teaching*.

National and Regional Sociology Meetings

The Section on Undergraduate Teaching sponsors variety of activities at national and regional meetings. These activities include formal sessions, roundtables, poster sessions and receptions. When I first began going to meetings in the later 1960s you had to hunt for sessions on teaching. Now, there are so many that you will find it difficult to attend even a significant portion of the activity. There is no doubt that teaching is back in sociology! The Section can be credited with the resurgence of teaching interest at our national and regional meetings.

There are other things you can do at meetings to support your teaching of the introductory course. First, be sure to visit the book exhibits at the ASA meetings. This is a quick and efficient way to see what is going on in textbook publishing. Usually there are book representatives as well as home office editorial workers who can provide you with information on forthcoming textbooks and the supporting ancillaries.

Other exhibitors can be helpful to you with your introductory teaching. Many specialized organizations have booths at the national meetings and can give you information. For example, good information for teaching can be obtained from the Census Bureau or the staff of *Sociological Abstracts*. There are also booths that exhibit hardware and software for teaching. The regional meetings sometimes have exhibits but they do not achieve the quality of the national meetings.

Teaching the Mass Class

In closing this section of **TIPSTEACH**, I want to discuss some things related to teaching the mass class which I define as any introductory class over 250 students. It is likely that you will not get direct responsibility for such a class. Given the pressures on staff in sociology departments, you might be asked to take on the responsibility of teaching the mass class. If you do, don't panic - there is help available.

First, go to a colleague who has taught a large section. This person likely will be happy to talk with you about some techniques that he or she developed while teaching the mass section. But be prepared for some war stories which will sound terrible, like students reading in class, sleeping in class, or walking out of class during a lecture.

Second, buy the ASA handbook edited by Reece McGee entitled *Teaching the Mass Class* (Second Edition). This volume has a wealth of information for both the beginner and veteran of the mass class. McGee has also done a short film on teaching the mass class.

A latent function of teaching the introductory course is the opportunity to reach publics outside the classroom. This is the topic of the next section of TIPSTEACH.

REFERENCES

Cashin William E. and Victoria L. Clegg. 1994. "Periodicals Related to College Teaching" Idea Paper #28. *Exchange* Kansas State University: Center for Faculty Evaluation and Development. pp. 3-7.

McGee, Reece 1991. *Teaching the Mass Class*. Second Edition. Washington, D.C.: American Sociological Association Teaching Resources Group.

SECTION ELEVEN
LIFE OUTSIDE THE INTRODUCTORY COURSE

Introduction

The sociologist should be engaged in the life of the community beyond the classroom. As an introductory teacher you will be in contact with the widest range to students than any other of your colleagues in the sociology department.

Social Role of the Teacher

William McKeachie (1978: Chapter six) drawing on the work of Cytrynbaum and Manning presents a typology of six roles for the teacher. The six roles logically come to gather in two categories. The first category has to do with knowledge function of teaching. In the knowledge category are the roles of **expert, formal authority** and **facilitator**. The **expert** is charged with the responsibility of teaching the central concepts and theories of the field. The **formal authority** plays the role of the gatekeeper in the education process who must set education goals and procedures for reaching those goals. Lastly, the **facilitator** promotes student creativity and growth. The role has to do with the professor's responsibility for helping students set goals. McKeachie suggests there are three roles that train the student including the roles of **socializing agent, role model** (called ego ideal) and **person**. The **socializing agent** acts to clarify student goals and career paths. The **role model** responsibilities of the teacher are enormous. McKeachie says the professor conveys to the student his or her excitement for the discipline. Lastly, in this category, is the professor as **person** or human being. McKeachie proposes that in the person role, the professor reveals himself or herself to the student. In revealing oneself to students as a human, one validates the "human" in the student. All of these roles are present at one time or other in the classroom, but they also appear outside the classroom.

Life Outside the Classroom

The professor has so many roles, as McKeachie's typology clearly suggests. In addition, in the introductory course, you will come into contact with a wide range of students, probably greater than in any other sociology course. Indeed, this accounts for some of the fun of teaching "Intro". Because of this, you will likely be asked to do a variety of things outside the classroom. Whether you do them depends on your time, energy and self-image as an academic. In this concluding section of **TIPSTEACH,** I want to write about five things that you may be asked to do which are not strictly related to the classroom activities, but do fall under the rubric of the various described above. These activities include helping students with research projects, brokering student services information, writing letters of recommendation, participating in social activities and talking with the media.

Helping Students with Research Projects

As an introductory teacher you will run into a wide range of students who will ask you for help. These requests can be as simple as a citation request or as complex as actually participating in the project.

The first type of request is the seeking of information about a topic that student is working on in another class. Usually this request is fairly situational in that the student hears you say something during a lecture and that triggers an idea for a research question.

The second type of request is reviewing research questionnaires. This can be tricky. The questionnaire is likely to be fairly simplistic. If you are too critical you can discourage the student. But not being critical will be seen as your approval of an instrument that is, in fact, of poor quality. So try and gently point out the weaknesses of the instrument.

The third type of involvement is actually being in the student project. Once I was interviewed by two of my students who received an assignment from an English professor to interview an older person. (Ouch!) Another time a photography student asked me to toss a toy soccer ball around the studio for an hour.

There are two rules that you should follow in working with projects with students. One, the student should clearly indicate your involvement in the project to his or her professor. Two, the project should not interfere with the work that you are currently doing in the class. Parenthetically, you will likely get requests from former students to get involved with projects.

Helping students with their research topics can be a wonderful time to communicate the sociological imagination to students. As both expert and formal authority, you can show students how the sociological imagination works. Sociology tries to understand the intersection of the history and biography by using social theory and methodology. When working with a student on a research project you can teach the student the work of our discipline.

Brokering Student Services Information

The introductory teacher is likely to be asked for information that falls under the category of student services. You will become a broker of student services information. So be prepared to know where campus resources are located (Whitford, 1992). These may include such things as accessing student records, going to writing and tutoring centers, and even buying concert tickets. However, your most important activity in this area is getting students into counseling. This may range from suggesting a student go for some counseling help to actually walking the student over to counseling services. The best thing you can do is familiarize yourself with the various services available to the student. A good place to start is with your college or university's new student orientation programs as we become facilitators trying to help students on their own terms.

Writing Letters of Recommendation

You may not know a student very well. However, you may still be asked to write letters of reference. This can be a burden on your time. You should not neglect this responsibility. Most of the letters will be job related, particularly jobs within the university or summer jobs. For the most part you will be asked to address your student's character and work habits in your letter. Try and get the student to discuss the job with you before you write the letter. If you have the job in mind as you write, it will make a smoother and more coherent letter. One piece of advice: As your mother used to say, "If you can't say anything nice, don't say anything at all". It has been my experience that negative comments in letters of reference have a much greater impact than do positive ones. If you feel you have to write a negative comment, you might disqualify yourself from rewriting the letter. As letter writers, we play the role of professionals, particularly when in regard to the mechanics of the letter. Take care with the grammar and content. Most importantly, try to get the letter in on time, although as I write this sentence, I am thinking about my own sins in terms of deadlines.

Participating in Social Activities

Because of the range of students in the introductory class, you are likely to be asked to participate in many social activities as a university representative. Some are fun; others are a burden.

Let me explore a few with you. You might be asked to speak to groups in dormitories on some subject that you have mentioned in class. This can be very interesting, but time consuming. A brief half hour presentation can present a day's work when you figure in preparation time as well as the time before and after your talk.

You may be invited to participate in social programs as a guest of one organization or another. This is typically a one-shot affair and can be quite interesting. Your students will likely appreciate your involvement.

A more complex involvement is to become an advisor to a student group. This can be rewarding because it gives you a real feeling for the student culture. However, it can also be quite time consuming so be sure to find out the expectations of the group you are being asked to advise.

Talking with the Mass Media

You will likely be asked by student journalists to do radio, TV and/or newspaper interviews. If you do it, this can spin off into interviews with other local and regional media. In 1993, two of my doctoral students who are strong introductory teachers, Scott Reid and Jon Epstein, did interviews with a variety of local, regional, national and international media on their deviance research.

The basic interaction between a sociologist and a journalist is the interview, which is, essentially a structured conversation. Questions are always open-ended, raised with an assumption that clear-cut answers exist and will be forthcoming.

Despite "journalist objectivity," the journalist's questions seek confirmation of a pre-existing point of view. When a reporter, whether they are a student or a professional, approaches a subject, he or she is generally asking for a view to be confirmed or rejected. Disagreeing with a reporter's view can be tantamount to infanticide.

Gaye Tuchman (1978) makes a very useful distinction between three types of news: spot, developing and continuing news. Spot news is typified by a fire - a staple of regional newscasts - but tornados and earthquakes also qualify. Developing news is the breaking news story that has emerging facts and interpretations. The Branch Davidans in Waco Texas is a good example. Continuing news is a series of stories on the same subject. For example, the saga of President Clinton's health insurance plan fits this definition.

The sociologist, when called by the press to answer questions, should determine what type of story is involved. Reporters, either students or professionals, treat every story as spot news because they are working under such terrible deadlines - this is true of university news services as well.

When responding to a reporter, the sociologist can look less than knowledgeable if he or she responds to a story defined as continuing news when it is actually a developing story (rarely do we get involved with spot news). For example, I once responded to questions about a court's action related to the May 4 tragedy using the reporter's summary of the decision. I treated the story as a continuing one but in fact the reporter gave me a very narrow interpretation of the judge's decision and much more information emerged making my answer seem confusing and inarticulate.

Sociological analysis tends to be reserved from the third "graph" from the end of the story. Our remarks are the coda for interpretation. This is not pejorative, but an appropriate role for the sociologist. Sociology's approach to social structure and cultures can move the reporter away from the narrow micro approach often taken by journalists.

It is seldom imperative that he, the sociologist, respond immediately to a reporter's questions. The reporter should be asked three basic questions before the interview begins. The first is, "What do you want me to comment on?" I generally have no problem with questions about soccer violence but I feel uncomfortable with questions about rock concert violence. When a reporter or radio producer provides you with details about what he or she is interested in, this often gives you an opportunity to shape the interview as you wish or choose not to be interviewed at all. It allows a chance to do some preparation for the interview.

Two, "Have you talked to any scholars?" The answer to this question can signal whether or not a reporter or producer is serious, or using the lone sociologist as a "universal" academic to balance the story. Sometimes, you will be referred by other scholars on campus or off. But, generally there is only academics on the story. Thus, the sociologist is well-advised to tell the reporter that you are not prepared to talk at this time, but you need some time to think about the issues. When not answering immediately, you should always try to set an interview date within the next twenty-four hours to answer the questions. Third, "What have you read on the subject?" Most reporters and radio producers will be calling you because of something they have read. There is probably no single morning radio talk show producer in America who does not read *USA TODAY*. Having this kind of popular material in hand can be helpful in bringing a common frame of reference to an interview. For example, I was once was asked to do a radio interview based on an interview I gave to the *LA Times*. Since I did not have the *Times* article, I asked the radio producer to FAX it to me, which she did and the radio personality based the interview almost completely on the article.

Sociologists are uniquely positioned in the university to play this external role. It is a wonderful opportunity to teach the sociological imagination beyond the classroom.

REFERENCES

McKeachie, W. J. 1978. *Teaching Tips: A Guidebook For the Beginning College Teacher*. Lexington, Mass.: D. C. Heath.

Tuchman, G. 1978. *Making News: A Study in the Construction of Reality*. New York: The Free Press

Whitford, F. W. 1992. *Teaching Psychology*. Englewood Cliffs, New Jersey: Prentice-Hall.

SECTION TWELVE
CONCLUDING THOUGHTS

The second best job in the world is being a college professor of sociology. The best job is playing second base for the Chicago Cubs! In this monograph I have tried to share with you my experience and research on teaching the introductory course. As I said at the opening, there is no more important course than "Intro." Yet we have too often neglected it for the glamorous upper-division and graduate courses. I hope this monograph contributes in a small way to correcting that neglect.

Emile Durkheim, as quoted in Goldschmid and Wilson (1980: ii) said, "Pedagogy depends on sociology more closely than on any other science." This quote suggests a natural link between sociology and teaching, teaching and sociology. Yet, for some reason, there seems to have been a separation between doing sociology and teaching it. Nothing could be further from the truth. If the professor will simply be a sociologist in the classroom commenting and analyzing the social world in the way we are trained to do, the teaching will naturally follow. This is not to say that preparation and technique are not needed. Of course they are! It is to say that in my view, sociology is very teachable. Because of this, with some training, enthusiasm, and a little luck it is fairly easy to bring this terrific discipline to your students. There are many students who await the sociological imagination. I call them SOSs, or Souls for Sociology. Go for it! It has been nice talking with you.